MISSIONARY KID

How I Learned to Say Goodbye

MISSIONARY KID

How I Learned to Say Goodbye

John Haines

with a few drawings by the author

For Dorothy, a missionary kid,
and for all you Innocent Ones

CONTENTS

PROLOGUE
THE LADY IN THE DJELLABA

Casablanca, early May. A busload of tourists has just rolled into town. English-speaking tourists. Some from England, others from Canada, South Africa and elsewhere. The majority from the United States.

It is lunchtime. The passengers are hungry. The bus stops at a café on the Boulevard de l'Océan overlooking the Mediterranean Sea.

Not a cloud in the sky, it's a picture-perfect day. But these tourists are tired. This is their last day on a week-long tour of Morocco. They are tired, sick from eating too much food and driving too many miles. It is time to say goodbye to Morocco. They tumble out of the lime-green bus, looking for bathrooms and a quick lunch.

"You have one hour," says the tour guide.

Two couples, one Canadian and the other American, find a restaurant and sit down at a table together to order their meal.

If I had to describe these two couples to you, it would be difficult, since all North American middle-aged tourists look the same, especially the men. The

1

sunglasses. The brightly colored shirt. The neatly trimmed salt-and-pepper beard. The loose khaki shorts that look comfortable because there is a tag inside that says "comfort waist."

Two white middle-aged men, one on either side of retirement, each one with their middle-aged wives.

They order their meal, and the one middle-aged man, the pre-retirement one, decides to find a restroom. Where is the restroom? Down the stairs, sir, just on your right.

The man makes his way down the stairs. He has a cold. He is already thinking of his home in Canada, of sitting on his deck with a comforting beer.

In Morocco, as in many countries in this world, one finds in most public restrooms, right inside near the entrance, a traditionally dressed woman in charge of cleaning the place, and, not far from her, some kind of small container for tips.

In this case, it's a little glass dish.

Like the middle-aged man, this woman is no different from the rest of her kind. She wears a simple full-length dress – a djellaba – and on her head some kind of turban. At least that's what it looks like. Zigzag patterns of brown henna cover the back of her hands, on the part close to the wrist. Probably when she smiles, if and when she decides to smile, there will be a gold tooth somewhere.

The middle-aged man passes her.

She looks familiar, like someone he knew from long ago, but he can't think of whom. He goes to the bathroom.

He walks out and drops a few coins – Moroccan dirhams – into the little glass dish.

"*Shukran*," he says, which in Arabic means "Thank you."

Not bad for a middle aged white Canadian man.

Actually, not that impressive. After an entire week in Morocco, the least one should be able to say is *shukran*.

Still, the woman smiles. And, sure enough, there's the gold tooth.

But then, she does something that a traditionally dressed cleaning woman from Morocco seldom does to a white middle-aged male tourist.

She stops him with a question.

"*Wash kat 'arif al 'arabiya?*" – meaning, "Do you speak Arabic?"

Something about the way he said *shukran*, maybe. Or maybe something else. She asked him if he speaks Arabic, so something must have made her think this.

The man, almost out the door, stops, and now she sees. His simple "thank you," his last word to a Moroccan lady before flying out early tomorrow morning, was more than just a tourist's perfunctory *shukran*.

"*Wash kat 'arif al 'arabiya?*" she asks.

"*La, walakin...*" – "No, but..." he answers.

Here the man waffles, he tries to gesture with his hands. He's forgotten how to say "a little bit," even though he has practiced it often in the last week.

This woman, she reminds him of another woman, a Moroccan woman from fifty years ago, a maid from Salé who, when this man was just a baby fifty years ago, cradled him in her arms. This woman did this, every day. Every day for the first two years of his life.

Zohra was her name. Zohra, fifty years ago. Right here in Casablanca.

The middle-aged man is still waffling.

"*Bishwya*," says the cleaning lady, helping him out. "A little bit." Again, she smiles.

The middle-aged man wants to tell her how he feels, what it means to him to have met her at this very moment, just before saying goodbye to Morocco. He wants to tell her that she is like a mother to him, even though she's a complete stranger, that she is both like a home to him and a foreign land. He wants to tell her how happy he is to meet her and how sad he will be when, seconds from now, she will be gone.

'*Ummy*, he wants to call her. '*Ummy*, mother mine. But he doesn't know the words. All he can do is repeat *bishwya* after her.

"*Bishwya*," he says with a smile. That's what he meant to say, that he only speaks Arabic a little bit. *Bishwya*.

"*Shukran bizyef*," he adds as he leaves. "Thank you very much."

He would like to say more, he would like to ask this woman if she knows another woman, a woman probably no longer living by now. A woman by the name of Zohra. But there would be nothing to say.

A thousand Zohras live in Casablanca. A thousand Zohras have died in Casablanca. And, without her last name, how could he ever find her?

You may have guessed by now that the middle-aged man in this story is me, John Haines, the son of American missionaries who came to Morocco fifty years before.

And the cleaning lady?

I never did get her name. Who knows? Maybe, just maybe, her name was Zohra.

PROLOGUE, TAKE 2
MY NEIGHBOR MIKE

Next door to me lives one of the nicest couples I have ever known. They do not go to church, nor do they profess to be Christians. Mike and Dorothy are just hardworking citizens, married for fifty odd years. They raised two sons, gave them everything two boys could ever want, and these sons in turn gave them four grandchildren.

I never cease to be amazed at Mike and Dorothy's devotion to their grandchildren. They attend their school events with religious devotion and have framed pictures of all four on their wall.

One evening not too long ago, I was walking my German Shepherd dog Tessa, when I ran into Mike and Dorothy who were out for a stroll.

"And how are the grandkids?" I asked, followed by, "Tessa! Off!"

This is how most conversations go with Mike and Dorothy, since my dog Tessa likes to jump on them. I know that this is bad dog behavior, but Tessa means well. She just wants to play. Usually, Tessa wants Dorothy to throw a stick so she can catch it.

"I don't have a stick, sweetie," said Dorothy to my dog Tessa.

"They're fine," Mike said in answer to my question about the grandkids, as Dorothy patted Tessa several times on the head. Mike is a man of few words. So, when Mike says the grandkids are fine, they are absolutely fine.

"The eldest one is in the Ringettes," Dorothy offered.

All I could think of when I heard the word Ringettes was the Rubettes, an English band from the seventies whose hit "Sugar Baby Love" was one of my favorites as a kid growing up in France.

"What are the Ringettes?" I asked.

By this time, Tessa had started chasing her tail.

For those of you who have never witnessed a dog chasing its tail, allow me to describe it to you. There are times when my dog Tessa sits quiet and alert. At other times Tessa lies down. This is what she is doing now as I type this sentence. Only if it is loud enough does a noise make her  raise her head, as you can see in this picture I have drawn of her. But even then, she is only pretending to be vigilant. Pretty soon Tessa's head eases back down, her eyelids close and all of the noises of the world fade away.

Except, of course, if the phone rings, which just happened, and so I must end this paragraph.

At other times, Tessa is agitated, as when standing next to Mike and Dorothy, and this is when  the chasing of the tail threatens to begin. Her mouth opens slightly. Her eyes glaze over. Her back begins to arch. The chasing of the tail is about to begin. Once the chasing of the tail is in full swing, it is hard to describe or even depict, but I have tried to do so in this picture. When chasing her tail, Tessa becomes a blur of fur. She can hardly keep up.

Where was I?

Oh yes, my question to my neighbor Mike about the Ringettes, which was interrupted by Tessa chasing her tail.

"You don't know what the Ringettes are?" Mike asked in response to my question. Now, when Mike, a man of few words, asks a question, it means that he is genuinely worried.

"No," I muttered.

Dorothy then proceeded to explain to me about the Ringettes, but I didn't catch much of what she said. What I couldn't stop thinking about was their granddaughter's good fortune to have both of her doting grandparents present while she played Ringettes.

How I envy Mike and Dorothy's grandkids!

By the time I was four, I had only seen two of my grandparents. My maternal grandmother Minnie Dickinson, whose story you will hear later on in this book, came to visit us in Casablanca when my sister was born. I was two at the time, and one of the pleasures of getting  to know Grammy Dickinson was listening to her read to me. I loved to listen to Grammy's stories! A few years later, my paternal grandfather came to visit, my Grampy whom you will also hear about later.

Only when I turned five did I finally see all of my grandparents for the first time – one of only four times before I turned eighteen.

Visits to my grandparents were dictated by the three-year intervals of my parents' return to their home country. My second visit with my grandparents was when I was nine, the next when I was twelve and the one after that when I was fifteen. No sooner had a visit with my grandparents begun than it was time to say goodbye. Goodbye, always goodbye!

I miss them now, but it is too late.

As I think back on those years, and then look across the way to my neighbors' grandchildren, I am struck by the main difference between me and them. The difference is that I am a missionary kid.

The expression "missionary kid," I think you'll agree, is peculiar. "Missionary kid" is an American phrase that came into vogue around the Second World War, by which time there were enough of us American missionary kids to warrant a nickname. "Missionary kid" is one of those cool American expressions: it sounds shallow but packs a clever punch, the sort of thing that we Americans love.

Like "Hula hoop" or "Ivy league." "Hula hoop" sounds playful, like "whoopee" – exactly the way you feel while Hula hooping. The serious part is "Hula," some ancient Hawaiian dance, if I'm not mistaken. As for "Ivy league," it's fun but profound, just like American academics.

"Missionary kid," on the face of it, is shorthand for "a missionary's kid," or, to put it even more awkwardly, "a child of missionaries." "Missionary kid" sounds fun and serious. You're a kid, that's fun. Your parents are Christian missionaries. Less fun.

"You're a missionary child," a colleague of mine used to tell me when I was living in the State of Georgia. He himself was a preacher's kid.

"No, I'm not a 'missionary child'. I'm a missionary kid," I protested.

"Nah, you're a missionary child, brother," he insisted in that overly familiar tone that religious people often adopt to assert themselves. "A missionary child doing the Lord's work."

Missionary child! Switch those two words around and you have "child missionary."

Missionary kid = Kid missionary.

So, needless to say, many of us missionary kids do not like the expression "missionary kid," and even less the shorthand "MK." Would you want to be saddled so early in life with your parents' profession? Maybe, but at least you'd want to be given the choice.

There is another reason for our dislike of the missionary kid label. Although they didn't used to be, many of our own missionary parents are now wary of the word "missionary."

Recently, I was sitting with a missionary and his wife.

"So, do your fellow missionaries–" I began, but the missionary didn't let me finish. "We don't use that word," he interrupted. "We prefer the term 'workers'." Turns out he was worried that his apartment was being bugged, which it probably was.

The point I'm trying to make here is that the word "missionary" has become less and less popular since my childhood, even with missionaries. In the 1980s, my parents' mission removed the word "mission" from their name and replaced it with "ministries" in order to better deceive foreign governments.

We missionary kids learned early on to tuck away the word "missionary" and replace it with something else: "expatriate," "pastor," "tentmaker," "hobo jetsetter."

Anything but missionary.

Some people even started taking the word "missionary" out of "missionary kids." Not that long ago, a few well-intended people with PhDs started calling us "third culture kids" instead, and when they got tired of that, they called us TCKs.

Somebody even recently called me an ATCK. I have no idea what that means.

It doesn't help that many people nowadays think of Christian evangelical missionaries as narrow-minded and even dangerous. I don't know what you make of that missionary couple in Barbara Kingsolver's *The Poisonwood Bible*, but I for one am very glad I was not one of *those* missionaries' kids. The one died of a snake bite and the remaining three fled to the far corners of the earth to escape their parents, a lunatic father reviled by the natives and his own family, and a mother so broken by work that she ended up institutionalized.

I've known a lot of missionaries in my missionary kid life, but none of them as unlikable as that missionary couple in *The Poisonwood Bible* – which, incidentally, is a great novel. But it's a novel. A novel written by someone who is neither a missionary nor a missionary kid.

Even evangelical insiders conspire against missionaries. In his book *Crazy for God*, missionary kid Frank Schaeffer, whose father Francis Schaeffer we all considered one of the coolest missionaries around, portrayed his Dad as a self-obsessed, sex-obsessed train wreck.

Not so much crazy for God as just plain crazy.

And never mind my fellow academics, especially anthropologists (which seems to be everyone I know nowadays), who reserve special scorn for Christian missionaries. According to them, missionaries are the bigots of history, the main ones responsible for that wicked thing called colonisation.

The other problem with "missionary kid" is that many of us are no longer kids. We used to be, but we aren't any more. And although we're the same persons as our childish selves, our views and life circumstances, like everyone else's, have changed.

What's more, if we're old enough, our parents, like mine, have retired from missionary service. They're no longer missionaries.

For many missionary kids, the days of thinking about missionaries and their kids have long passed.

Me, I used to hate the expression "missionary kid." I was ashamed of it! For most of my life I never referred to myself as a missionary kid in public. Or I replaced it with something else. Like "hobo jetsetter," which by the way is my own creation.

But there's something about turning fifty that forces many of us to reckon with our past. As a historian, I have spent a lot of time writing up other people's lives, and the last thing I wanted was someone else doing that for me. Too many twists and turns, too many opportunities for someone else to get it wrong.

I have written this book for three types of people, lists of three being a feature of the sermons I grew up on.

The first group is made up of those who know about Christian evangelicals and their missionary activity, and generally support it. Let's call this group the Believers.

If you are one of the Believers, then I want to thank you, because without your monthly financial support I could never have afforded that skateboard or four years of boarding school.

The second group let's call the Unbelievers.

Unbelievers are familiar with missionaries and their shenanigans, and they don't like them. Let's be honest, some of these Unbelievers are Disenchanted Missionary Kids, let's call them DMKs, of a certain age. You likely will not hear from DMKs because they decided long ago to have nothing more to do with anything related to missionaries – including a book entitled *Missionary Kid*.

Whoever you are, whether Unbelieving reader, DMK or some other disenchanted soul, thank you for reading these words, and know that I have great sympathy for your point of view. I too have multiple copies of Philip Yancey's *Disappointment with God* that were given to me by concerned Believers.

If you didn't get that last literary reference, then you are a member of a third group of readers, those for whom I have written this book. I was going to call you the Unreached, but really you are the Innocent Ones. You are innocent of religion, of evangelical missionaries and their kids.

Maybe, Innocent One, you even thought that a "missionary kid" was a toddler evangelist. And that's OK, because in your innocence, you couldn't have known any better.

Know that it is for you especially, Innocent One, that I have written this book about my life.

Know that I mainly had you, Innocent Reader, in mind, someone like my neighbor Mike. Mainly what you should know about my neighbor Mike is that he is anti-religious.

This is how my first conversation with my neighbor Mike went.

"Hi, I'm John," I said.

"Hi John," he said, "good to meet you. I'm Mike."

At that point, we both paused because, as I told you earlier, Mike is a man of few words.

"We've just met," Mike continued, "so I should probably tell you that there are three things you should know about me."

He paused.

Then he said: "I don't smoke. I don't drink. And I don't do religion."

Mike stopped to see what effect these words would have on me.

"I have no problem with any of that, Mike," was all I said.

And from that moment on, I knew that Mike and I were going to get along.

Maybe you are wondering which one of these three groups I belong to? Am I one of the Believers, who openly supports Christian evangelicals and their missionary evangelization of the world? Not really. Am I an Unbeliever, a DMK who wants nothing to do with missionaries and their shenanigans? Nope. And for sure I'm not an Innocent One, since, as I told you, I have been inundated with religion from day one.

No, I am neither a Believer, an Unbeliever, nor an Innocent One.

Well, alright, there is a fourth category of persons I haven't yet mentioned, a whole separate tribe.

Missionary kids, just plain missionary kids.

Me, I'm just a missionary kid.

PLANTED

CHAPTER 1

THE PERSUASIVE

DR. STEELE

Nothing in my parents' background indicated they would be evangelical, born-again missionaries. Their parents weren't missionaries, nor were their parents' parents. No, my Mom and Dad were run-of-the-mill American teenagers of the fifties. They went to the movies, drank Coca Cola and danced to rock 'n' roll music. There was, however, a kind of wound or longing in each case that prepared both of them for that most important moment, the moment when they became born again.

Being born again like my parents was something that we missionary kids did not experience.

It was something we missionary kids *could* not experience. From the moment we exited the womb, we were bombarded with evangelical Christianity. After all, my parents' job description was to turn Muslims into born-again Christians.

No, we missionary kids were never given the chance to smoke, drink and dance, and generally enjoy a life of dissipation. Growing up, I figured that it sure would have been nice to smoke, drink and dance like my own parents had before they became born again!

I was having lunch with a lesbian colleague of mine when this question of being born again came up. (We missionary kids love to sound as secular as possible, which is why I informed you just now that my colleague was lesbian.) Judith, my lesbian colleague (there, I just did it again), has a heart of gold. She has taught me a lot over the years.

"So, Judith, do you want another martini?" I asked her. (We missionary kids love to pretend as if we were raised by normal, cocktail-imbibing people like our grandparents rather than by our evangelical tee-totalling missionary parents.)

"No thanks," she said, "I'll stick to wine for the rest of the meal."

"John," my lesbian colleague Judith said to me as I took another sip of my martini to prove how secular I was, "you've talked about your parents' experience. But how about you? Were you ever born again?"

I nearly dropped my martini.

Hearing this question from my lesbian colleague threw me for a loop. A secular lesbian professor asking me, a missionary kid, whether I had been born again!

"Wow, that's a good question, Judith," I answered. "I don't know."

For months afterwards, I was troubled by Judith's question. I racked my brain. I pored over old letters and diaries. Surely my missionary parents, whose sole purpose in life was evangelism, had made sure that their own children were born again!

Alas, I could find no trace of my being born again. I began to worry. I finally broke down and asked my retired missionary mother.

"Mom," I said, "I'm assuming I asked Jesus into my heart as a little boy. When did that happen?"

"Sorry to let you down," she answered, "but that event doesn't ring a bell." No kidding. Those were her very words.

Uh-oh. So, I was not born again!

"But," she hastened to add, "I will never forget your baptism in Germany or that time when you burned all your rock 'n' roll tapes."

Whew! So, I *was* born again. Sort of.

Still, I was dumfounded at the flimsy evidence for this missionary kid being born again. Dumbfounded, but not surprised.

We missionary kids never understood why normal people, including our parents, had behaved like heathens for years before finally converting. How unfair! From day one, we missionary kids were forced to behave. My Mom's own Dad got away with waiting to become born again until most of his life was over. After seventy-four years of wallowing in his heathen ways, he woke my grandmother up in the middle of the night.

"What about eternity?" he asked her. My pious grandmother explained to him that – and here I am quoting her directly – "the Lord is just waiting for an invitation to come into our hearts," as she doubtless had many a time before.

But this time, the old man figured, well, I'm seventy-four, so I'd better do this now rather than tempt fate any further. So, he prayed the prayer of faith and that was that. All seventy-four years of heathenistic dissipation, dismissed. Me, now in my early fifties, I would still have another two decades of wild hedonism left if I had followed my grandfather's example!

But no. Our parents made sure that we missionary kids prayed and read the Bible all the time, as soon as we came out of the missionary womb. In fact, our spiritual wellbeing was indispensable to our missionary parents' job.

Now, after all that, I should come clean.

I should confess to you – Believer, Unbeliever and Innocent One – that I have no children of my own. I have no idea of the challenges faced by young parents, and especially by young missionary parents in the 1960s. I'd wager, though, that few missionary parents back then cared for their two little kids, body and soul, with more love and devotion than my Mom and Dad, John and Margy Haines. And this was because John and Margy loved each other as desperately as two human beings likely ever have or ever will.

But that's just my opinion, and I'm just a missionary kid. You, reader, will have to judge for yourself.

In one of his first French conversations in Morocco, my father committed an especially embarrassing verbal faux-pas. Sitting with my mother in a French class, he introduced the two of them by uttering the following sentence:

"Je suis sudiste, et ma femme est nudiste."

What my father was trying to say in English was the following: "I am a Southerner and my wife is a Northerner."

But, to the amusement of his French teacher, what he ended up saying was: "I am a Southerner and my wife is a nudist." I suppose that Dad's statement was accurate, since my parents probably didn't conceive me with their clothes on.

It was also true that Mom and Dad came from two separate worlds. Theirs was the union of North and South. My Dad, John Haines (confusing, I know, but I was named after him), was the youngest of two boys raised in Petersburg, Virginia. As the impish junior, Dad loved to tease his older brother Bob and generally get up to mischief. Dad's  proclivity for prankishness continued well into his adult years, and occasionally got him into trouble.

To illustrate this, let me tell you the Coconut Story.

As a young missionary in Morocco, my Dad decided one day to tease a single-lady missionary named Betty Eveland by placing a coconut in front of her apartment door early one morning. Now you should know that Miss Betty, like many missionaries back in those days, lived in a poor section of town. In fact, Miss Betty lived near a brothel. Anyways, the coconut that Dad had placed in front of Miss Betty's door was hollow inside except for a single sheet of paper on which were inscribed the following words:

I'M NUTS OVER YOU.

– A secret admirer

Unfortunately for my Dad, one of Miss Betty's neighbors happened to be with her when she discovered the coconut in front of her door.

"C'est une bombe, Madame," said the alarmed neighbor. She then said: "Appelez la police!"

No matter how poor your French, I think you probably know what that means. In no time, the Moroccan police came in to tackle this bomb-in-a-coconut. They carried it out into the middle of the road, and slowly opened the coconut in order to defuse the bomb. But all that they found inside was a note that read:

I'M NUTS OVER YOU.

– A secret admirer

"Traduisez, s'il vous plait, Madame," a police officer said to Miss Betty, asking her to translate the note.

There is no exact French equivalent for "I'm nuts over you," but Miss Betty did the best she could. "Je suis fou de vous," she replied. "Signé, un admirateur secret."

Now, I did tell you earlier that Miss Betty lived next to a brothel. The police officer began looking at Miss Betty, a single-lady missionary, with great suspicion, wondering about the identity of this secret admirer who had left a coconut at her door.

"But she's not that kind of lady!" protested the neighbor. "She's a missionary!"

Needless to say, when Miss Betty found out a few days later who was responsible for the coconut, she had a few choice words for this John Haines – short of swearing, of course, since she was a single-lady missionary.

I have told you this story to illustrate my father's mischievous sense of humor, so let's return to his story, if you don't mind.

Dad's carefree, prank-filled childhood was shattered when his mother was diagnosed with schizophrenia. To cover up for his pain, my father turned to joking and, later on, even a little drinking. As Dad later told it, he seemed to be going nowhere.

It was at a meeting of the Intervarsity Christian Fellowship on the University of Maryland campus that my father became a born-again Christian.

That night, a recently converted gambler named Don Rosenberger was speaking. Mr. Rosenberger used a dollar bill to illustrate the Gospel message.

"What would you do if I handed you this bill?" Mr. Rosenberger asked my father.

"I would take it," my father replied. That very night he prayed the prayer of salvation and became a born again Christian. After that, my father stopped drinking and playing rock 'n' roll music. He had been born again.

Now, Intervarsity's tactic at the time was that, no sooner a student converted than he should be enlisted to convert others. A few months after his conversion, it was my father's turn to do what Mr. Rosenberger had done for him.

In the spring of 1958, Dad was giving his testimony at an Intervarsity meeting. Sitting at that meeting was a brunette by the name of Peggy Dickinson. John had no way of knowing that this woman would soon settle on him as the husband of her choice. Being found by Peggy would prove to be as life-changing a thing for John as conversion.

Peggy's parents Lee and Minnie Dickinson hailed from that part of the Canadian province of Nova Scotia that lies opposite to where tourists flock. Even in the summertime, Amherst, Nova Scotia, was, and remains to this day, quiet and uneventful. Lee had met Minnie in a one-room schoolhouse in nearby

Fenwick. He was a teenage farmer's son and she was his teacher, older than him by four years.

"I was sixteen and she was twenty," was how Lee remembered it years later. "I was on the side lines when she came to the evening socials. I would get sort of an electric shock even if I got a smile, and was touched by love."

My Canadian grandfather Lee was not one to emote. But when he felt something like being "touched by love," well, he felt it alright.

My mother Peggy, the youngest of three children, was not so much clownish as restless, and not so much restless as resolute. My mother's will was  then, and remains to this day, a force of nature. From her mother, Peggy inherited a hankering for travel, and from her father a desire to leave her hometown of Germantown, Maryland as quickly as possible. As a teenager, what Peggy wanted most of all was to walk out of her father's grocery store and into high society, literally across the tracks from her house.

When the time came for her first year at the University of Maryland, Peggy was determined to join a sorority. In what I believe was the only time in her life that Peggy's will was thwarted, her newly converted older sister, already enrolled at Maryland, banded with their pious mother to impose an exceptional one-year moratorium on sororities for young Peggy. Reluctantly, Peggy began attending Intervarsity meetings instead.

John's testimonial that auspicious spring evening in 1958 must have been persuasive. In true form, Peggy's conversion was instant and complete. She never turned back.

Mom used to say that she settled for Dad over more eligible suitors, including Intervarsity's popular leader at the time, a man who years later wound up in prison for sexually abusing his foster son. John and Peggy found in each other the one deficient parent. For him, a woman so perspicacious she could read people's minds, and for her an emotional artist who made her laugh.

I should probably explain to you Innocent Readers how one can be a prospective missionary and a romantic lover at the same time.

As new evangelical converts, John and Peggy couched everything in a spiritual language that prevented them from doing the more foolish things that most of us did back when we were young and in love. True, their love letters were filled with the usual sappy declarations, like "I think I'll burst if I don't write you" (my mother) or "you're a sweetie, Miss D." (my father).

Beyond such romantic outbursts, these two young evangelicals of the 1950s assumed that God was leading their every action. That is how a love letter could begin with "Hi cutie!" and end with "Loads of love in our Savior."

And so, a few years later, John and Peggy were married. How everything seemed right in that moment! From conversion to Bible School to marriage to signing up as missionaries, it took only four years, and suddenly they were ready to go.

It was only a matter of where.

By this time, Peggy had switched to her present name, Margy, a formality that signalled the seriousness with which she took her career as an evangelical missionary. Becoming a missionary in those days was a lifetime decision. My parents would be sent to the frontlines of God's elite soul-saving army.

They nearly went to South America. Here's how it happened. A few years before, five young missionaries had flown into the rainforest of Ecuador to meet up with a remote tribe on the Curaray River. They were never heard from again, but their bodies were soon discovered floating down the Curaray. The entire incident would have become yesterday's news had it not been for one of the five's widow, an enterprising writer named Elisabeth Elliot who turned her husband's martyrdom into the bestseller *Shadow of the Almighty*, a real page turner. My impressionable father devoured *Shadow of the Almighty* and immediately started packing his bags for South America.

Luckily for me, John was disabused of the idea of saving the savages of Ecuador. This was the first of several happy Twists of Fate without which I would not have become a missionary kid and written this story. This first Twist of Fate determined my birthplace.

For if my parents had gone to Ecuador, I would not have been born on the exciting continent of Africa where David Livingstone was once nearly eaten by a lion, as you can see in this picture. Nor would I have gone to France, which later in life gave me much needed cachet. Neither would I have attended the Black Forest Academy and met the love of my life, as you will hear later on.

No, instead, my father would have been murdered in the rainforest, and I would have been home-schooled in the wild by my widowed mother and then forced to attend Alliance Academy International in Quito, Ecuador. Thank God, Al Hamdu lillah, Fate rushed in at the last minute in the form of a tall man who looked like a cross between a clown and an archivist.

This man's name was Dr. Steele.

Dr. Steele, as we all called him, was one of a handful of people, along with Billy Graham and Moses, that my mother spoke of in the way that Catholics speak of the Pope.

Dr. Steele's word was infallible.

Dr. Steele was the U.S. Secretary for the North Africa Mission, a small English outfit in need of new missionaries.

Dr. Steele had the panache and authority of a professor. When he spoke, he kind of chewed on his words which made them run together with a little splashing sound in the background. I still remember Dr. Steele years later, an eccentric old man who could pull one story after the other out from that remarkable head with its overactive eyebrows and wispy hair.

Dr. Steele was a very persuasive man.

Thanks to Dr. Steele, John and Margy Haines were persuaded to become missionaries with the North Africa Mission. Once they agreed, they had less than a year left before their departure.

Considering the traumatic adjustments that lay just around the corner, their training was risible by today's standards. Candidate School, as it was called, consisted of two weeks with Dr. Steele on a farm in Pennsylvania. It was a hodgepodge of Bible study and presentations on the Muslim world, with a psychological test thrown in to make things modern.

Whether the bucolic scenery or the histrionics of Dr. Steele prompted it, I do not know, but sometime in that two-week period, I was conceived.

Six months later, with me in my mother's belly, we were on the boat to Morocco. The weather was awful, and my pregnant mother was forced to sleep in third class. But none of that mattered to two young missionaries with a lifetime of adventure before them.

The pastor who months earlier had commissioned them, summed things up with a witty phrase, as pastors are wont to do.

"Three people are going for the price of two tickets," he said.

CHAPTER 2
ZOHRA

I was born in the sixties, the proud son of American missionaries to Morocco. It was the best of times to be an American missionary in Morocco, and it was the worst of times.

Sprouting up towards Europe like a cowlick on Africa's crown, the Kingdom of Morocco has beckoned visitors for centuries. In the 1960s, there were lots of them. They came for the scenery, as did David Lean for his *Lawrence of Arabia*. They came for the music, as did Brian Jones for his *Pipes of Pan at Joujouka*.

They also came for the heathen.

By 1960, a handful of Christian missions were active in Morocco. The most prominent of these was the North Africa Mission and its outpost, the Tulloch Memorial Hospital in Tangier.

Tulloch Memorial was run by two English doctor missionaries, Drs. Farnham and Janet St. John. St. John, by the way, is pronounced "Sinjun" like "Injun." Dr. St. John oversaw my birth, and Tulloch was home for the first few weeks of my life.

My parents belonged to the North Africa Mission's new American cohort. From Montana to Virginia, these young Americans had come to save Morocco from the clutches of Islam.

They had also come to save the North Africa Mission from obsolescence.

Led by Dr. Steele with his overactive eyebrows and wispy hair, the American contingent pumped new blood into the English mission. The early 1960s marked North Africa Mission's highest number of recruits ever and since: one hundred and twenty-five missionaries spread out across the Maghreb, with a concentration in Morocco.

The Americans had won the Second World War, but a new battle for souls was on!

More mundane problems were brewing in Morocco, however, problems that would eventually expedite my missionary family out of Morocco five years after we arrived. These problems had started long before.

When in the 1800s Europe was squabbling over who would get which slice of the African pie, it was decided that France, on account of its proximity and general greatness, deserved most of North Africa. But then, after France's flogging in World War II, all hell broke loose. One by one, each land of the Maghreb declared its independence. First Libya, followed by Egypt, Tunisia and Morocco.

By the time I was born in Morocco, a storm was gathering. Its name was *Istiqlal!*, the cry that now rang out all across North Africa: "Independence!"

"**V**ous avez un fils! ("You have a son!"), declared the French nurse assisting Dr. St. John (yes, that's "Sinjun") as I exited my mother's womb. Because a typhoid epidemic had broken out at Tulloch Memorial, Mom had to give birth to me in another hospital in Tangier, a hospital named, I kid you not—

Clinique Californie.

The problem with the name Clinique Californie (literally, "Clinic California," as in "Hotel California") is that it sounds like bad French. Although most place names in Tangier have been changed from French to Arabic ones since the time I was born, this clinic has retained its French name – with a twist. It is now called California Clinique, written in large Arabic letters on the front of the building:

كاليفورنيا كلينيك

Some of you Believers are getting nervous just now because I wrote something in Arabic, but there's no need to be nervous. It's just Arabic for "California Clinique," which sounds nice and American.

A few days after I was born, the typhoid epidemic at Tulloch Memorial passed, and Mom and I were transferred out of Clinique Californie.

My parents named me after my father John, but mostly called me Johnny. I was my parents' first child, once again thanks to a Twist of Fate, the second such twist in my story.

34

For I had nearly been the middle child. A couple of years earlier my mother had miscarried. If this child had survived, I would have been second in line, and thus would never have possessed the supreme self-confidence of a firstborn, and consequently you would not be reading this book that I have written about myself.

As some of you Innocent Ones and Unbelievers already know, the firstborn believes him or herself to be at the center of the universe. Let me give you an example of this. As a baby in Morocco, one day I started coughing for no reason. My parents thought I was sick until they realized that I was simply enjoying this new sound. Not only did I revel in the inflections of my speaking voice, I even loved the sound *of my own cough*. For those of you non-firstborns, this is ridiculous. Not so for us self-obsessed eldest children.

It turns out that all I was doing was practicing my future professorial clearing of the throat.

What, you may wonder, especially you Innocent Readers, does a missionary actually do? Well, basically, a missionary's job is to convert as many heathens as possible so that these heathens don't have to die and go to hell. In my parents' case, the heathens were Muslims.

Having arrived in Morocco, my missionary parents found no shortage of handy heathen. The problem was communicating with them. So first they had to learn the heathen tongue. Thankfully, my parents, two fresh-faced Americans with virtually no previous experience in a foreign country, were motivated not only by their evangelical fervor, but by something even more compelling.

The glamor of Arabic.

"We love to hear the people speak their Arabic in its fascinating guttural tones," my father wrote to his parents a few days after his arrival in Casablanca.

So, Mom and Dad went to work. Every day, they took lessons in both Arabic and French. Thankfully, because she was a missionary living in Africa, my mother had help in caring for me, her only child. This was because back then missionaries working in Africa had one indispensable time-saver, a relic from colonial days:

The indigenous household maid.

To give you an idea of how different things were for missionaries in other countries, during her first decade in Germany, my mother-in-law Elinor lived in a one-bedroom apartment with a hole in the floor and no heated water. (Now is probably as good a time as any to confess that I, a missionary kid, married another missionary kid.) Every day, during the cold months, Elinor had to walk up and down four flights of stairs to fetch buckets of coal so that she could heat her apartment and bathe her two young children in a large pail not far from the said hole in the floor.

Elinor had no maid to assist her.

By contrast, for most of her five years in Morocco, my mother, like many married missionary ladies living in Morocco at the time, oversaw her maids like Scarlett O'Hara in *Gone with the Wind*.

"We invited a Moroccan Christian and two other fellas to our place for Saturday supper," she wrote to her family one day. (No, I did not make that sentence up, she actually used the word "fella." Even sounds like Scarlett O'Hara.)

"I had Zohra make a tajine that morning for four men," Mom continued, "but somehow by the time the evening arrived, we had eight around the table!"

My Mom then turned into a frenzied Southern matron, and joined Zohra and Aziza in the trenches.

"We worked frantically in the kitchen to have enough. Aziza had come with a pan of harira, so I served that first, then the tajine for four, and while they were eating that, I threw together a huge salad with Russian dressing... It ended with tea and Moroccan pastries." And yes, in case some of you Believers are wondering, especially you Southern Baptists, that was *sweet* tea. Very sweet, hot Moroccan tea.

Our maid in Casablanca was named Zohra.

The name Zohra, which in Arabic means "flower," is as common in Morocco for girls as Mohammad is for boys. In Casablanca alone, where we were living at the time, there were likely thousands of Zohras.

In fact, over the course of my family's five years in Morocco, we got to know several Zohras. These Zohras were distinguished by their last name. Our maid Zohra was Zohra Salaouya, meaning "Zohra from Salé." Later on, there was a Zohra Rabatya, which, as you've probably guessed, means "Zohra from Rabat."

This last Zohra, Zohra Rabatya, was a converted Christian. But our maid Zohra Salaouya was not. Maybe Zohra Salaouya was too stubborn, or maybe my parents' Arabic was not yet good enough. Whatever the reason, she managed to resist conversion until I was about three years old. Secretly, I suspect, my mother worried about having to leave every day for  language study while Zohra, a Muslim woman, took care of me.

But the fact is, I didn't mind Zohra at all. If you must know, I loved Zohra very much. She and I spent a great deal of time together for the first two years of my life. Zohra and I shared many secrets, none of which I am at liberty to reveal in this book.

Most weekdays for the first two years of my life, while my parents went to language classes and missionary training, Zohra shopped, cleaned and made the meals. Zohra took care of me as if I were her own son, for she was a widow with no children of her own. To this day, I consider Zohra my second mother, my Moroccan mother. In Arabic, the expression is *'ummy*, meaning "mother mine." In Arabic, *'ummy* is written like this:

Decades later, when, sitting in a psychiatrist's office, I started the daunting process of rummaging through the attic of my past which ultimately led to this book, the first thought that came bursting through, like a sacred and long forgotten light, was Zohra.

Like a song, Zohra came shining through!

Sometimes in my mind, quietly to myself, I sing to Zohra, to remind me of my Moroccan roots.

Zohra, second mother!

Zohra, mother mine, *'ummy*!

Zohra, keeper of my heart! During our days together, how did you hold me?

How often you must have leaned in and whispered in my ear!

What songs did you teach me, songs in our language, songs buried inside me, waiting to resurrect? What secrets did we keep, you and I?

Zohra! Long after our two years together, the first two years of my life, fifty years later and fifty years too late, I came back and once again breathed the air of Casablanca, but I could not find you. How could I have found you since you were probably not alive?

Are you, still alive?

Forgive me, *'ummy*! Forgive me, and if by some miracle you still walk among the living, if by chance you get wind of these words, then hum our secret song, and somewhere I will sing it, somehow I will hear it, you know that I will!

Zohra, *'ummy*, know that I am here and that I have never forgotten you.

On Morocco's west coast, facing the Atlantic Ocean, lies the kingdom's most storied city, Casablanca. Hugging the ocean is Casablanca's medina, walled in to keep the new things out. Radiating inland from the medina, until Casablanca ceases to be Casablanca and eventually becomes the High Atlas Mountains, sits the city proper and a street that today is called Zenqa Al Banafsaj.

In the 1960s, the Zenqa Al Banafsaj Street was known as the Rue Bugeaud, named after a French general who back in France held the dubious title of Le Marquis de la Piconnerie. The Rue Bugeaud was the North Africa Mission's hub where both language classes and church services took place. Further south, within biking distance of the Rue Bugeaud, on the outskirts of Casablanca in a neighborhood known as the Quartier Polo, were the residences for young missionaries and their families.

While my parents spent their days at the Rue Bugeaud conjugating Arabic verbs and naming household objects in French, Zohra and I whiled away the day in the Quartier Polo.

Missionaries are sometimes called expatriates. Expatriate literally means someone living outside the Fatherland (*ex patria*), and this was true of Mom and Dad. They had left America, but they continued to remain faithful to their Fatherland. They read *Time* magazine. They ate Jello pudding. They played Blockhead and wore the Mohair sweaters sent to us by American supporters.

Over time, my expatriate parents did learn to love a few other Fatherlands besides America. Slowly Morocco sank its hooks into their hearts.

It all started with couscous.

Someone once said that the way to a man's heart is through his stomach. They couldn't have fathomed the power of the couscous grain. This tiny fleck of wheat has seduced the hearts of millions.

Couscous, the national dish of Morocco, is served simply, in a dish with vegetables and some

41

meat on top. Sounds simple, but the secret lies in the making. Here again, my family's indigenous servants proved to be useful.

"Today we had the Moroccan national dish," my Dad wrote to his parents soon after his arrival in Morocco.

"It is couscous," he explained, "very small rice-like affairs topped with meat, 'chic-peas', raisins, and vegetables – plus gravy, and all eaten from the same bowl."

"Margy and I are just crazy about it," he continued. "When and if we are able to get our Moroccan maid, we'll have her cook it as only they can." In time, Zohra was making couscous for us regularly.

Some two years later, on the day of America's most important religious feast, Christmas, we were all seated on the floor of our Moroccan apartment eating our new favorite dish.

"We like it even better than couscous," wrote my father.

It wasn't couscous Dad was talking about this time, but another dish called tajine: potatoes topped with meat and dried vegetables, each bite scooped up, not with the silverware of the civilized, but with the cutlery of the heathen: warm, fresh bread.

As for me, up until the age of five, Morocco was all I had ever known. Not only Moroccans – Zohra and others with whom my parents spent time – but my parents' tightknit community of American missionaries.

For these expatriates living far from their American home, evening gatherings, week-ends and holidays were all spent together.

Pictured here is one such occasion, a birthday party at the Rue Bugeaud. My mother stands holding me. Sitting down on the right is a missionary couple, George Rider and his wife Ann Rider, the woman in the white blouse.

At Mrs. Rider's feet sits one of her four children, Kenny. Kenny Rider, like his father, has a winning smile. Next to Kenny on the floor, sitting at my mother's feet and wearing a white hat, is the Riders' eldest, Sarah. She has curly black hair and, like her brother Kenny, that winning Rider smile.

And, at the left-hand corner of the picture are the other two Rider kids, Ginger and Billy, both wearing hats and about to break into their winning Rider smiles.

You will notice, if you turn back over to Ann Rider, that her belly protrudes slightly. The reason is that, at the time, Mrs. Rider was pregnant with her *fifth* child.

Five missionary kids!

For a financially strapped missionary couple working in Morocco, the feeding and caring of five was... well let's just say, it was lots of money.

Perhaps, Believer, and even some of you Unbelievers as well, may judge the Riders for having had so many children. (I sense that you Innocent Readers are withholding judgement.)

But be merciful, if you can, Believers and Unbelievers. Consider that these children were the only cousins and playmates available to me at the time, creatures that were then, and have since remained, my one true kin.

Missionary kids.

CHAPTER 3
IT WAS ALL
JOY'S FAULT

A little over two years after I was born, my parents announced in one of their Prayer Letters that we had moved from Casablanca to Salé, a suburb of Rabat. They also announced the arrival of a newcomer in our financially overextended family of three.

My sister Joy.

"You'll doubtless want a closer view of our little daughter, Joyce Frances," they glowed. Next to a photograph of the squirming infant was the caption, "here she's about a month and a half." I am showing you the picture they included in the Prayer Letter so that you can see for yourself. If you compare this baby to the baby I recently showed you (me), there is no question as to which is the best looking one.

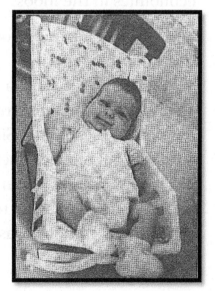

Now, you Innocent Readers have been patient until now, but I believe the time has come for me to explain to you about the Prayer Letter.

You Believers and Unbelievers are snickering, because you know about the Prayer Letter. So, I think it would best if you tuned out for a moment or went off to have a snack.

Let's wait a moment, Innocent One, for the Believers and Unbelievers to clear the room.

Now that we are alone together, the time has come for me to tell you, Innocent Reader, about the missionary Prayer Letter. But before I can explain to you the Prayer Letter, I should probably cover, as rapidly as possible, the basics of missionary economics in the 1960s.

The main thing for you to know is that most missionaries survived on paper checks from supporters in America. These supporters were rewarded for their generosity with regular updates of missionary service. Since the internet was not available, missionaries sent these updates in the form of a letter. And this letter, Innocent Reader, this letter in which missionaries recounted their activities of converting heathens, was known as—

The Prayer Letter.

In the annals of the colonial literature so fanatically studied by university students nowadays, how sadly neglected is the litter's forgotten runt, the lowly missionary Prayer Letter, the highly readable, the highly entertaining Prayer Letter!

To be fair, the Prayer Letter should have been called the Money Letter. For its main purpose was not so much to update our American supporters so they could pray, as to ask them for the one indispensable thing:

Money.

It was OK if we had no converts to show for any one given month, but money was the one thing my missionary family could not do without.

Prayer Letters read in some ways like a communiqué from the US Army. Missionaries went overseas on the "field." They were split into small "teams." Teams assembled for "councils." There was the "Prayer Council" and the "Field Council." Every three years our missionary family was allowed a "furlough" of leave from duty, at which time they first reported to "headquarters."

Actually, the main inspiration for the Prayer Letter was the Bible, and especially the letters of the Apostle Paul. A Prayer Letter would begin with a Pauline phrase like, "Dear friends in Christ" and end with "Yours in His Grace." As a missionary kid, I was exposed to the Bible  from the very beginning, as you can see from this picture. For better or for worse, the Bible shaped the way I viewed the world then, and it has continued to influence me right up to the present day.

There would be more to say about the Prayer Letter, but I can see, Innocent One, that your eyes are glazing over, so please call the Believers and Unbelievers back in.

～

Now that you have returned from whatever you were up to for the last few pages, Believers and Unbelievers, I will recount the events that led to my sister Joy's birth which caused our family's exodus from Morocco.

Having completed their language training, my parents attended the mission's Field Council meeting at the Regional Conference in Casablanca. Strategies were discussed, teams proposed, and the field commanders decided that we would go to Rabat.

"We have been assigned to the bookstore in Rabat, the capital of Morocco," my parents stated in a Prayer Letter.

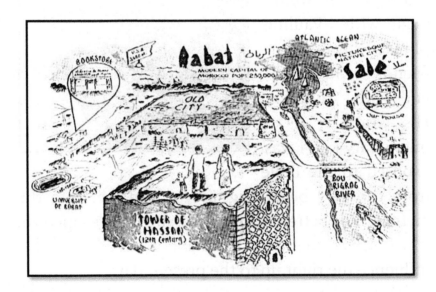

A few Prayer Letters later, my Dad made one of his cartoons depicting us newly arrived in Rabat, which you can see on the previous page. On the right, you have the city's northern end, where the Bou Reg Reg River separates the Old City from the suburb of Salé. At the southern end of Rabat, in the city proper, sit attractions such as the Tower of King Hassan. My father has depicted our family of three atop the Tower of Hassan, gazing out at the city, with him holding my hand.

It is a picture of true missionary happiness.

Yes, our first few months in Rabat were happy days. Everything was going so smoothly! Even our maid Zohra, my beloved 'ummy, had come with us. I was one happy missionary kid! But then, something terrible happened.

No one was exactly sure how the troubles began. But I knew. Our troubles had been caused by Joy. For the first two years of my life, I was my parents' only child, the object of their attention. And then, in August 1966, my mother brought home from the hospital a baby, apparently hers. And now apparently *ours*.

That was when the bad times began. They started as soon as Joy was born and did not let up until two years later, when our family had to flee Morocco with all our possessions like the Children of Israel on their way out of Egypt.

First came trouble at the bookstore, my father's new evangelistic assignment. The bookstore was located downtown Rabat on the Avenue Jean Jaurès. It featured various kinds of Christian literature displayed on elegant book shelves, as you can see in this picture. To leave no doubt as to the purpose of the bookstore, a giant Bible was painted floating on the wall above the book shelves. The idea was to lure people in from the street and convert them once they found  themselves confronted by a large Bible floating above them. "The store sells all kinds of Christian literature in Arabic, French and English," my parents wrote in a Prayer Letter, "as well as office and school supplies." Clever decoys, those office and school supplies!

A more delicate issue was what to call the bookstore. The sign on the Avenue Jean Jaurès in Rabat read "Librairie La Bonne Nouvelle," which in French means "The Good News Bookstore."

The name had a good ring to it. Plus, it was ambiguous. No one would know what kind of news it was – maybe Christian, maybe Muslim, or maybe just plain old good news – until they walked into the bookstore, and then they would see the large Bible painted on the wall and my father coming towards them.

At first the Moroccan authorities were deceived. They paid no mind to this good news bookstore. For good measure, the bookstore's name was also plastered in Arabic script on the main sign outside, in big letters like so:

مكتبة البشارة

In Arabic, this reads, "Maktaba al-bishara." Literally, "Bookstore of the Good News."

This name, I think you'll agree, was way better than "Christian Evangelical Proselytization Center Run by American and English Missionaries for the Conversion of as Many Muslims as Possible." Still, it wasn't long before the authorities found out what kind of news my father was peddling and shut the place down.

A few months after Joy's birth, Dad began to feel tired.

"Sometimes," my mother wrote, "John comes home exhausted from trying to summon forth his very best Arabic in an afternoon's conversation."

Clearly, my father's exhaustion, too, was caused by Joy's arrival.

Then, a few months later, only six months after Joy was born, several of North Africa Mission's directors were called in to be questioned by Moroccan police. "You must stop all anti-Islamic proselytism!" they were told in no uncertain terms.

After that, more and more missionaries were called in to police headquarters – including Miss Betty, on whom my father had played the coconut trick I told you about earlier.

This persecution by the Moroccan police was followed by other setbacks, including the government's shutting down of the mission's Christian camp at Khemisset.

Around this time, my family was forced to move out of the luxurious villa in which we lived, a villa with a handful of servants and a nice little dog named Jolie in the cushy suburb of Salé. We were forced to move to a dank apartment in downtown Rabat where we all got sick.

As if this wasn't enough, exactly a year after Joy's birth – hardly a coincidence – my parents visited a missionary kid boarding school in Tangier named the Bethel School. As you Believers know, and some of you Unbelievers as well, Bethel was the place in the Bible where the wicked King Jeroboam forced the Children of Israel into worshipping a golden calf.

There, at the Bethel School in Tangier, I was going to be sent off to board very soon, although my parents did not tell me exactly when.

"We saw Bethel," my father wrote. "We were very impressed with both. I think Johnny will have to go there, but I really don't mind after seeing their good setup," Dad continued.

All of this was compounded by my family's general discouragement and financial woes.

"Recently," my father wrote, "Margy and I had about come to the end of our rope in finances. Ever since coming to Rabat we have been short and struggling to make ends meet."

There seemed no end to the trouble caused by Joy's arrival.

Then came the final blow. The earthquake. Mom had just left with Joy for Tangier to have the little darling's tonsils taken out, when my Dad and I awoke in the middle of the night to a 7.3 magnitude earthquake.

Like the tenth plague that propelled the Children of Israel out of Egypt, this earthquake shook us up so badly that we left Morocco. Four months later, on the eve of my fifth birthday, we boarded a plane in Casablanca and said goodbye to Morocco. It would be another forty-five years before I was to see the land of my birth.

Feb 1960
agadir

Eventually I did come to like – I believe the right word is love – my little sister Joy, my only sibling. It was not easy at first. For starters, there was the matter of my sister's cost. More than once we had to remind supporters of this financial burden.

"Our monthly support figure is $470.00," wrote my parents in a Prayer Letter, addressing their supporters as "Dear Friends in Christ" – not *that* dear, since they weren't giving us enough money.

"At present, we are lacking $35.00 of this figure, due to Joy's increase in our support." The tactful phrase "Joy's increase in our support" actually meant "the extra financial burden on our support caused by Joy."

In addition to Joy's financial cost, there was also the emotional cost on me as the firstborn.

"Johnny has his ups and downs getting along with Joy," wrote my father to his parents when I was three and my sister one.

"Today he bopped her over the head with a little car he got for his birthday. But she still gurgles with joy when she sees him first thing in the morning."

At some point, however, I must have given in and learned to share things with Joy rather than bop her on the head with them. Not only things, but people too, like my friend Bouazza, shown here holding both of us in Rabat. Yes, little by little, things did get better between us.

Not too long ago, over forty years after the events related in this chapter, I wrote a song for my sister Joy. It goes like this:

Sister Joy,

Your name doesn't rhyme with any word that

Makes it easy to sing a song about you, sister Joy ...

Sister Joy,

Where does the time go, go away?

It leaves me singing about you,

Sister Joy.

Back when I was five years old and my sister was three and we were living in Morocco, I never imagined that someday I would cry as I am doing now, just thinking about my sister Joy.

Over time, something happens to the missionary, exactly what is hard to say. On returning to the States after five years in Morocco, my parents discovered that, not only had they changed, but so had America.

"We were a bit amused at the way we Americans are so 'busy,'" they wrote in a Prayer Letter after returning to the States.

"There is much leisure time, and so many amusements unheard of in simple Morocco... People are so absorbed in gadgets, the latest fads, selfish cliques."

A kind of distance from America had set in. A kind of vanity, too. "Often lately," my father wrote in his diary during his Morocco years, "I have been tempted to think I'm pretty wise: after all, I know French and Colloquial and Classical Arabic!"

Dad had ceased to be an ordinary American. He had become a multilingual soul-saving missionary. This condescension towards Americans with their "gadgets and fads" that my parents now felt, we missionary kids felt it too. We missionary kids were just as exceptional as our missionary parents!

They no longer belonged in America, and neither did we.

And so, we figured we would go on forever to live like them the glamorous life of hobo jetsetters, looking down our noses at America which had never been our home in the first place. We too were destined to be holy people crisscrossing the Atlantic, moving seamlessly from one continent to the other.

Like a wedge, Morocco had come between us and America. Like a siren, Morocco beckoned us. The breeze coming off the Atlantic on a summer morning. The music of Arabic spoken at a midday souk, blending with spices and sweat and a soupçon of urine. The taste of couscous in the evening, as it goes down the gullet and, steady as a flame, raises the tempo of the beating heart.

Not to mention the people of Morocco. The American missionary does not mix with the wealthy but with the poor, who are more susceptible to conversion. In Morocco, there are the poor, and then there are the really poor. A picture my father took during our Rabat days, while on a trip deep into the Moroccan interior, shows a barefoot mother with her two children. The oldest, a boy, clings to his mother's tunic. It  was people like these whose stories my parents listened to. Not too long ago, a Moroccan friend of mine looked at this picture and cried. I realized then that, although I never was that boy, I have always felt as if I knew him very well.

I don't remember much from our first American furlough. I attended kindergarten in New Jersey and did not do well. I played with other missionary kids. I waited for my parents' next assignment. I was ready to take my leave of America.

When we finally found out where we would go next, I was thrilled, although I didn't know a thing about the place. It was a city named Marseille.

CHAPTER 4

OF BULLIES
AND BRAS

If you visit Marseille today, you will likely reach this city in the South of France by train after spending a nice week-end in Paris. Fresh from your nap, you will hop onto the subway, stroll over to the History Museum, then mosey back to the Radisson "Blu" hotel after a relaxing meal on the Vieux Port. And if you like it enough, you will purchase a vacation property nearby, paid for by the book you will write on your adventures in Provence. That's assuming you are English.

This, however, was not the Marseille I knew.

In 1970, there was no TGV, no subway, no History Museum and no Radisson. The Vieux Port was grungy and its hotels dodgy. Marseille was called "Le petit Chicago."

The reason for this? An unprecedented surge of immigration and poverty in the 1960s.

After a century of being colonized by France, the people of North Africa were granted legal status to work in the same nation that had raped their homelands. They came by the tens of thousands. And the funnel through which all of these Maghrebi immigrants flowed into France was the port city of

 Marseille, an hour's swim away from the northern tip of Africa, Morocco's Cap Spartel where I had sat on a donkey at the age of one, as you can see in this picture. From Morocco, Algeria and Tunisia, they came to France to take the jobs no Frenchman wanted: street sweeper, janitor, garbage collector. They were crammed into towers called HLMs ("Habitations à loyer modéré," meaning "Moderately priced housing"). In short order, HLMs became the slums of France.

By 1970, the year my family moved to Marseille, there were over fifty thousand immigrants from the Maghreb in France, nearly all Muslims and most in Marseille's HLMs. The slums of Marseille were a Muslim-converting missionary's dream.

1967 Wilson

Thus began the "Marseille Offensive," as my father called it in a Prayer Letter. The ripest for conversion were the children. Poor and hungry, they often wandered the streets of Marseille after school (if they even went) before curling up at night somewhere in the overcrowded HLM that had become their temporary home. Their names were Abdul and Fatima, Jamil and Kinza, the faceless offspring of Europe's industrial slaves.

Marseille, as I have just described it for you, was the city of my childhood. I lived there from age six to twelve. After wandering from one continent to the other, I was finally home. Marseille became my hometown. By age seven, I spoke and wrote French fluently. English had become a second language which I now spoke with a southern French accent.

I will never forget my first day of French public school.

I was six years old. Our family had moved into an apartment in Marseille's immigrant-friendly thirteenth district. Whatever little French I might have learned in Morocco had disappeared after a year of kindergarten in New Jersey. As I made my way on that September morning to my new elementary school, I knew that I was about to be put in a room with strangers who spoke a language I did not understand.

With Mom grabbing my one arm and a teacher the other, I was dragged up the stairs to the room, crying and begging not to go. After a long struggle up the stairs, we came to the classroom. I walked in and was seated.

What exactly happened after that, I have since forgotten, but by the end of that year, I was speaking and writing French with such ease that I finished first in my class.

The credit for this goes to a teacher whose name I have unfortunately forgotten. This teacher was the third happy Twist of Fate in my life, without which I would have performed miserably in French school and never become a writer and never written this book.

Every day during recess, this woman sat me down and helped me with French, speaking carefully so that I could understand. I still have one of my exercise booklets from this time period. There, in the margins, sit her kind annotations. The page shown here begins with a writing exercise and ends with a short dictation. In the left-hand margin, my teacher's mark: *tbien* for "très bien," meaning "very good," an unusually high compliment. The

French used to say that a hundred percent was reserved for the Good Lord ("Cent pour cent, c'est réservé pour le bon Dieu"). So "très bien" meant just that. My work was very good, just like the Good Lord.

And so, presumably, was I.

For a time, my life in Marseille was very good indeed. I went to school and read lots of Bible at home. During daily family devotions, our family of four sang catchy hymns like "Heavenly Sunshine."

Me, I preferred popular French songs to hymns, songs like "Allô, Maman bobo." It's a song worth quoting, if only to disabuse any of you Innocent Readers who might have assumed that my childhood in France was spent reading Proust and reciting

Molière. I am almost embarrassed to translate "Allô, Maman bobo" for you, but here goes:

> I'm unwell in the country, and unwell in town, maybe I'm a little too fragile! Hello, Mommy, boo-boo! Why did you make me, I'm not good-looking! Hello, Mommy, boo-boo! Hello, Mommy, boo-boo!

Still innocent of rock 'n' roll, my musical world in Marseille was a weird concoction of "Heavenly Sunshine" and "Allô, Maman bobo."

But then something happened that put an end to this idyll.

Bullying has become an almost fashionable topic for discussion nowadays. Forty years ago, however, few were bothered by it. To this day the French have no word for "bully." In 1970s Marseille, bullying happened so often as to go practically unnoticed. As I prepared to enter the French third grade, my family made an unexpected move, and this was when I met my bully.

That summer, we left our little apartment for a sprawling villa. Dad was put in charge of our mission's new center which targeted North African youth. They were going to be enticed with games like table tennis (*le babyfoot*), rowdy Christian choruses accompanied by my Dad's guitar, and, the ultimate ruse, Arabic lessons.

That fall, I started third grade at a new elementary school. I settled in uneasily, focussing on drawing and daydreaming. My drawings impressed both teachers and classmates. One day, a boy approached me in the hall after art class.

"Fais voir ton dessin – let me see your drawing," he said.

He was older, with close cropped hair and light-colored eyes. The boy's question was less a request than an order, so I gave my drawing to him. It was the best one I had, and I don't believe I ever got it back.

The boy's name was Antoine Cilia.

Antoine – or Toinou, as his associates called him (like "Tony" in American mafia films) – was the school's established bully. He had been held back two entire school years, which in French school was the kiss of death. Surrounding himself with a posse of likeminded delinquents, Antoine Cilia ruled the playground at recess. His entourage was known as "Cilia's gang" ("la bande à Cilia").

For three years, Toinou was my bully. He only made vague and unfulfilled threats, just often enough that I wouldn't forget him. Not once did he touch me.

This was because I seldom gave him the chance. Little by little, I learned to avoid Toinou by making myself as invisible as possible.

Over three decades later, I was sitting in a psychiatrist's office undergoing some kind of hypnosis treatment. At one point, sitting with my eyes closed,

I was transported back to the old playground. Everything came back. I felt the straps of my *cartable* book bag and the feel of the pillars behind which I used to hide for the entire recess.

A few years before that hypnosis therapy, I had returned to the old school in Marseille. There I was, a grown man, standing in that playground, facing the shadowed area where I used to hide myself away behind the stone pillars, alone in my fear of Antoine Cilia.

That day, the playground was empty. All the boys of my childhood were long gone. But deep in my gut the fear still festered like a wound that never heals.

Eventually, three years after I first met Antoine Cilia, my torment came to an end. In the fall of 1975, I began *collège*, Junior High, and entered the sixth grade, *sixième*. That fall, I switched to a neighboring school and was suddenly free of Antoine Cilia. Still, the fear that he might lurk around the corner never left my mind.

One day, on my way back from school, he reappeared, sitting on a post as if he'd been waiting for me all day.

"Elle est bien, ta montre – what a nice watch," he said with a grin, pointing to the new ticker on my wrist. I hadn't seen Antoine Cilia for nearly a year. In a flash, all of my anxiety rushed back.

"Toinou," I moaned, the fear swelling up from my stomach to my throat.

Toinou just smiled, glanced at the watch and then patted me on the head, as if the whole thing had been a game. I laughed nervously and walked on, leaving him sitting there, and never turned back.

That was the last time I ever saw Antoine Cilia.

How, when puberty strikes, does a boy learn to look at a woman? How does a woman, assuming it's a woman and not a man the boy wants, become the object of his desire in the first place? These were tough questions for a missionary kid. When puberty started sneaking up on me, I was inspired by sources ranging from posters for the soft-porn *Emmanuelle* movies we saw on the way to church, to the Bible stories we read every day.

Mainly, the Bible taught us missionary kids that woman was created for man's enjoyment. The Apostle Paul, who apparently never lived with a woman, could afford to be opinionated about the female sex. Among other things, Paul believed that wives should be subject to their husbands. Obviously, the Apostle Paul had never met my mother.

We missionary kids also took note of our very own Adam and Eve. My parents demonstrated their  affection, although it was mainly Dad who instigated things. My sister and I knew from Dad's kissing of my Mom out in the open that a man's desire for a woman's body was not necessarily shameful. Even with his pre-teen children around, the ones sporting the symmetrical homemade haircuts seen in this picture, my father never failed to kiss his wife enthusiastically every morning. And I believe she enjoyed it, possibly reciprocated in private, who knows?

Dad even learned something from the French.

On one occasion, we had invited our pastor Monsieur Molinengo and his family to our home for dinner. A television show came on that featured "rather permissive scenes" and "some suggestive dancers," as my father related in his diary at the time.

"Look how well they dance!" exclaimed Pastor Molinengo to us children.

Dad was scandalized. But after giving it some thought, he changed his mind.

"We often feel the body is evil," he wrote in his diary, "whereas the French feel it is beautiful."

Like Morocco, France was changing my father. France had already changed me quite a bit when it came to thinking about ladies' bodies.

Television was to blame.

Mom hated French television. "Johnny was invited to the home of a little French boy," she reported back to her family one day, "and I fear his eyes were glued to the TV rather than playing."

When at Dad's insistence we finally purchased a television set, Mom insisted on as small a model as possible, one for which she sewed a thick leather cover to hide it when it was turned off.

When the television was on, I admit that I was hypnotized by both shows and advertisements. One advertisement was of special interest to many French men and boys, and to me as well. It was an advertisement for bras.

Invented by a nineteenth-century French woman for the purpose of titillating all of mankind, the bra, which the French call *soutien-gorge*, had by the 1970s become a staple in advertisements across the globe.

As always, the French advertisements were some of the most risqué in Europe. The chief bra company in France was called Dim, a name I will remember to my dying day. Dim advertisements featured a woman bursting forth into a very public place, wearing nothing on top but a bra. What made her even more enchanting was her musical accompaniment, a jazzy piece led by a catchy trumpet melody.

It turns out the Dim bra music was by an American composer, Lalo Schifrin, the creator of the theme for "Mission Impossible." Fond as I was of this TV show, you can imagine, Unbeliever and Innocent Reader, how attracted I became to the ads for "les soutien-gorges Dim."

The moment that little trumpet melody started up, however, my father would lunge at our tiny television to change the channel, which just made the event that much more exciting for me.

The solution of one fellow missionary kid's father to this dilemma was to place himself for the duration of the ad with his arms outstretched in front of the television.

Facing the television.

For an American missionary kid, the Dim bra ads were capitalist sex dished up French style: raw, chilled, with not a garnish in sight. The opposite, in other words, of American sex: all covered up with colorful doodads and so smothered with subterfuge as to pass for pietism.

Raised in pagan France by evangelical Americans, me, I was stuck somewhere between Marilyn Monroe and Brigitte Bardot, both of whom I knew mainly from hearing about them than from actually seeing their films. In the end, it didn't matter, since I ended up with neither. More of an angel-faced Marlene Dietrich, as you will soon hear.

In the fall of 1975, when I was eleven years old, my parents contemplated a move. Their work in Marseille was done. Fewer and fewer children were attending the youth center. We were going to have to say goodbye to Marseille.

Where next to sow the seeds of the Gospel onto the fallow fields of Muslim hearts? The mission council suggested Algeria, but my parents rejected that option, Hamduh lillah! If they hadn't, I would have been sent back to North Africa and forced to attend the dreaded Bethel School.

No, my parents wanted to stay in France, and so did I. After toying with the idea of Lyon, the mission council turned its sights on a nearby city, a city more in need of missionaries, a city with an expanding North African immigrant population and a large university.

The city was Grenoble, at the foot of the Alps.

By February 1976, it was official. We were moving to Grenoble. After finally finding some roots in Marseille, I was about to leave the only home I had.

One more time, I was going to be uprooted. What I didn't realize was how long the rootlessness was going to last.

UPROOTED

CHAPTER 5

THE STORY OF
TWO FRIENDS

Now hear the story of a boy who had two friends! The one was cool, loved by many boys and girls. The other was quiet, and had no playmates at all. In the end, the one friend was faithless. But the other, the true friend, was as constant as a star that shines, night and day, even when the sun has blocked it from view.

A few years ago, I was sitting at a café in the town of Aix-les-Bains, having lunch with the editor of one of France's leading regional newspapers, *Le Dauphiné Libéré*, when a man walked up to our table.

"It's the mayor of Aix-les-Bains," the newspaper editor whispered in my ear as he stood up. I put my wine glass down and stood up too.

"This is my friend – *mon ami* – John Haines, a professor at the University of Toronto," the editor said to the mayor as he waved his hand in my direction. I shook the mayor's hand, beaming my best professional French smile. "Vous choisissez bien vos amis," the mayor said to me as he left. "You choose your friends well."

I sat down and resumed sipping my wine.

It took a few moments for things to sink in, but eventually it dawned on me how wonderfully strange life is. My *ami*, a well-connected newspaper editor who had just introduced me to the mayor of Aix-les-Bains, had once been a very shy boy. So shy that I had worried that he was not cool enough, and so for a time, I left him for a cooler friend. I would have been too ashamed to admit it to the mayor of Aix-les-Bains on that spring afternoon, and even now it stings to say it, but there was a time when I was unfaithful to my faithful friend.

A true friend is hard to come by, especially if you're a missionary kid. As some of you Unbelievers and Innocent Ones know too well, in order to make friends you have to stay in one place. Unfortunately for us missionary kids, our families kept moving from one place to another.

My family was always saying goodbye.

By the time I went off to boarding school in my mid-teens, we had moved on average every one and a half years, living in six different cities spread out across three continents. We had no home.

Goodbye, always goodbye. We kept moving from one exciting place to the other, city after city, continent after continent, and with every move, we left it all behind. Goodbye to teachers, goodbye to friends, goodbye to problems. Saying goodbye was like a drug. No problem arose that couldn't be fixed by saying goodbye.

As sure as rain comes in spring, the time would come for us to move on. From the souks of Morocco to the suburbs of Grenoble we kept moving, my father cheering as my mother masterminded. Wandering like the Children of Israel in a land that was not ours, we never got to stop and savor one of life's most priceless commodities: friends.

"You can always make new friends," Dad said to me when we first moved to Grenoble. "Oui, mais ça prend beaucoup de temps," I replied in French: "Yes, but it takes a lot of time."

It was going to take a lot of time – nearly three decades after I first met him in a French classroom, to be exact – but eventually I would make the friend of a lifetime, my true friend, Guy Abonnenc.

After grungy Marseille and the ghost of Antoine Cilia, Grenoble, a ski-resort town nestled in the mountains, felt to me like paradise. It was in Grenoble that I made two friends. Their names were Guy and Daniel. Daniel came from a working-class family. Guy, on the other hand, belonged to that provincial upper middle class whose stories have filled many a French novel.

Of the two, Guy and Daniel, it was Guy I met first.

Guy was Catholic. For my very Protestant parents, this was a major problem since they believed that Catholics were going to Hell, along with Muslims and other heathens.

Although he wasn't looking for Catholics, Dad kept running into them throughout his missionary career. There was this priest in Morocco, "a very likeable, polite man," my father wrote in his diary, but then caught himself: "anyone who is true to the Catholic Church is under a curse!"

If the odd hell-bound Catholic showed up in Morocco, France was positively crawling with them. As a Catholic boy, my new friend Guy would have automatically been consigned to hell, but for one reason.

Guy's mother loved Americans.

She had been a young girl when American tanks rolled into Grenoble at the end of World War II and sent the Germans packing. I was an American boy, and so Guy's mother spoiled me rotten.

When I would visit Guy's home, his palatial house with its shiny floors and spacious garden, Madame Abonnenc – as I called her – would have everything ready for us. I remember the bike ride leading up to their gate like it was yesterday. Out of breath from riding up the hill, I would stop at the gate and ring the bell. The dog would bark, then the gate would open.

"Mon petit John!" Madame Abonnenc would say, waiting at the door, her apron still on after making a strawberry *gâteau* just for Guy and me!

Forty years later I came back to the old house, once again opened the gate and walked up to the large front door. There was Madame Abonnenc, waiting as always. Many years had passed, and so had Monsieur Abonnenc her husband. We both cried then, and I cry now as I write these words, for Madame Abonnenc died only a few months ago.

I first met Guy when I walked into my new classroom in Echirolles, a suburb of Grenoble. I was twelve, and had the forlorn look of someone who had said goodbye to one classroom too many.

"We have a new student today," said the teacher as I walked in. "He comes from Marseille, and his name is John Haines." (The French pronounced this Djôn Ha-ayénes.)

A few minutes later, Guy quietly sidled up to me.

"Bonjour. Je m'appelle Guy," he said.

"Bonjour," I replied. "Moi, c'est John."

And that's how it started.

As I recall, we didn't say much after that. Class resumed and we both turned our attention to the teacher.

In his gentle way, Guy had chosen me as his friend. To this day, I am not sure why. Maybe because he, like me, was an outsider. An only child, Guy was shy and a little overweight by French standards of the time. Me, I was an awkward American missionary kid with a weird name, Djôn Ha-ayénes. We seemed a perfect fit.

A perfect fit except for Guy's being Catholic. But I didn't mind that. If my friend Guy was going to hell, then hell couldn't be that bad of a place!

Among our activities at Guy's house, my favorite was cartoons.

Guy and I started our own cartoon series. We modelled it on the famous cartoon books of Astérix, as well other French cartoon magazines at the time, like *Spirou*. Our comic book was released just in time for Christmas. On the back cover, I drew a sailor

smoking a pipe with two large bubbles containing our names, Guy Abonnenc and John Haines, collaborators and by then fast friends.

Thus ended my first year in Grenoble.

My academic performance was tolerable except for the sciences in which I received a 9.5 out of 20, disappointing even by American standards.

I didn't much care, but likely Mom and Dad were concerned.

That summer, for my thirteenth birthday, Mom had Guy over to our house and offered him one of the  few things his parents couldn't have bought him: American chocolate cake, unavailable in France. The cake was in the shape of Schroeder, the pianist from the American cartoon Peanuts.

In the fall of 1977, I began *quatrième* or eighth grade. *Quatrième* was to be, unbeknownst to me then, my last year in French school. Something else unbeknownst to me also happened that same year.

Full-on puberty.

Adolescence stumped both of my parents. They found it deeply troubling. I suspect if I'd had children, I would have felt the same way. Recently my female kitten Molly began howling and displaying her posterior to my bewildered neutered male cat. I was even more bewildered than him. That night, Molly was quarantined and sent to the vet's the very next morning.  Now Molly sits peacefully staring at everyone, including our neutered male cat. No more howling and displays of her posterior. It's as if none of that ever happened.

In *quatrième*, I was beginning to notice girls because girls, like my kitten Molly, were changing. I myself was undergoing changes. Things were happening in my pants and brain that went beyond any King James Bible verse I had ever memorized.

Sometime in that year of *quatrième*, I met Daniel.

Daniel had girls on his mind, too, except that he was doing something about it. Daniel possessed something Guy did not. Daniel was cool. A debonair adolescent with dreamy, dark eyebrows and a nose just large enough to suggest a serious sex drive, Daniel had an artist's sensitivity and a devilish streak. I never took his picture at the time, but years later he sent me a photo  of himself with his little girl. He and the girl's mother had separated, and he had since lived with quite a few women, as he eagerly confessed.

More so than Guy, Daniel spoke cool French.

Daniel used expressions like *putain*, which means prostitute and incidentally is a very common French expression. As in, "Ah, putain! Il est vachement chouk ton skate, John," which literally translated in English is, "Wow, prostitute! Your skateboard is cow-like cool, John."

Daniel not only had a way with words but also with girls. In *quatrième*, girls came flocking to him. Me, I wanted to be like Daniel!

The beauty I had set my sights on was named Véronique.

"Does John want to go out with Véronique?" one of Daniel's girlfriends asked us once. It was painfully obvious that I did. But I knew that Mom would kill me if that ever happened.

"Bien sûr," Daniel replied for me, "mais il ne faut pas le dire: il ose pas" – "Of course, but don't tell anyone: he doesn't dare."

Brave enough to hang out with Daniel, I was too chicken to declare my undying love for Véronique.

Ah, putain!

Beyond his skills with girls and words, Daniel was a gifted artist. By the fall of 1977, I had switched drawing partners from Guy to Daniel. One of Daniel's favorite cartoonists was Gotlib, the creator of a French Disneyland on steroids. Together, Daniel and I made cartoons like those of Gotlib. The title page of one of our cartoon books featured the two of us sitting on a couch. It had Gotlib written all over it: animals and humans cavorting together, multiple speech bubbles,  and creatures with half-mast eyes pitted against bug-eyed ones like the zooming devil you see at the bottom of the page.

Once I had mastered the style of Gotlib, Daniel introduced me to another cartoonist even cooler than Gotlib. The greatest cartoonist of all, according to Daniel, was Philippe Druillet.

Druillet's art was a tortured cocktail of science-fiction and fantasy peopled by dystopic machines and bare-chested women. It was "très seventies," as the French say.

A typical page from Druillet's "Lone Sloane" series had two or three main panels, each one irregularly shaped, the whole backgrounded by a drawing so large that most of it took place off the page. That year in Grenoble, my cartoons started to look like the epics of Druillet's Lone Sloane – except for

the naked women. In the half page shown here, from a story entitled "Big Time," the two main frames are separated by a jagged edge across the page, and fused together on the far right by an enormous tree. Dark clouds gather in the sky; heavy smoke wafts up from the ground.

For once, I think all of you Believers, Unbelievers and Innocent Ones can agree. This wreaks of puberty-ridden angst.

Another one of my stories took place underground in the year 40,009. (Don't ask me why that exact year, but at least give me credit for making it far enough in the future that it still sounds like a long time away today.) The two main characters in this story, named John and Angela, are bracing themselves for disaster as they cruise in a subterranean ship. At one point, John learns of the death of his two companions. In a close-up, Angela approaches to comfort

him. With her right hand, she touches his shoulder; with her left, she gently pulls back a strand of her long hair. Her suit is so tight that she might as well be bare chested.

Somehow my mother must have seen these drawings. Although she never spoke to me about them, I suspect they were the last straw.

Mom still maintains to this day that I was sent to the Black Forest Academy in Germany, the main missionary kid school in Europe at the time, because I was flunking French school. It's true that I was doing poorly enough in math and science that it would have been impossible for me four years later to pass the dreaded baccalaureate exam – known as *le bac* – short of a miracle from God.

In the spring of 1978, a miracle from God occurred. Up until then, my parents didn't have enough money to send me to the Black Forest Academy. All of a sudden, funds were found. By the spring, it was decided. I would attend the Black Forest Academy that fall.

My eight-year stint in French public school had come to an end. Once again, it was time to say goodbye. On one of the last days before my departure for Germany, Guy came over.

"On s'est bien amusé," I noted in my diary: "We had a really good time."

Daniel was not invited, nor for that matter had he ever been invited to our home.

The next year, when I returned to Grenoble for summer vacation, I visited Daniel. He proudly announced that he had made love to a girl for the first time. He was sixteen.

By then, Daniel and I were growing apart. The baroque paintings of Philippe Druillet, "très 'has-been,'" as he put it, already belonged to the old-fashioned seventies, a decade that was rapidly fading from view.

Meanwhile, Guy patiently waited in the wings. Over the many years that followed, he and I kept in touch. We remained friends, *amis*, for the long haul.

Not too long ago, I was sitting with Guy and his wife Muriel at a restaurant overlooking the Lac du Bourget, not far from Grenoble. As I remember, it was at the end of a long meal, and their son Mathis was making videos of us with his father's camera phone. Their daughter Iris sat quietly, as she always does, well behaved just like her father. Guy, Muriel and I were talking about life, as the French often do, in a vaguely philosophical way. The topic turned to friendship.

"So," Muriel asked her husband Guy, "who would you say is your best friend?"

Guy thought for a moment.

"John," he replied.

"But you only see John once a year at the most," Muriel said. "How can you say he's your best friend?"

"I can't explain it," Guy answered. "But that's just how it is. John is the closest friend I have in the world."

I can't explain it either.

Maybe it has to do with the past and the things that lie dormant and grow without our knowledge. Something like that. Whatever the reason, I have no doubt in my mind that my friend of a lifetime, my *ami*, is Guy Abonnenc.

CHAPTER 6
BOARDING SCHOOL

Have you ever had to say goodbye, Innocent One? Have you ever had to say goodbye to a house or country, to a lover or friend whom you knew you would not see in a long time, possibly ever again? If you have, then you know that this goodbye is the hardest goodbye in the world, because when you come back, if you ever come back, this person or place will have changed beyond recognition.

You too will have changed.

And so, whether you know it or not, this goodbye is the last goodbye.

In the fall of 1978, my parents and I made the long drive from our apartment in Grenoble to the Black Forest Academy in southern Germany. My mother was resolute, my father nervous, and me, somewhere in between. When we finally reached the boy's dormitory in the tiny village of Bad Riedlingen, Dad and I stood  awkwardly for the picture you see here. Standing there in the hills of the Black Forest felt a little like one of our vacations in Switzerland.

This was no vacation, however. This was no normal goodbye.

When my parents finally drove away, I don't think that I cried. Then again, I don't remember much from that moment. I do know that I cried myself to sleep that first night. And the next. And again, the following year.

Between that day in September 1978, when I entered the Black Forest Academy as a scrawny fourteen-year old, and August 1984 when, as a young man I vowed to love and to hold the woman to whom I am still married today, there elapsed a little less than six years.

At fourteen I left my childhood behind.

By American standards, boarding school in a foreign land at the age of fourteen is a hard way to begin adulthood, but it could have been worse. At the Black Forest Academy, I joined other missionary kids whose weaning had started years before, in the dorm halls at the Dalat International School in Malaysia or in the classrooms of the Rift Valley in Kenya. From hardened boarders to home schoolers, from diplomat and military kids to missionary kids, we all poured into the little academy at the Black Forest and fell into the beds of its dormitories.

Of all the kids – diplomat kids, business kids, military kids – we missionary kids were the worst!

There was the older Craig, who raised such a ruckus that he got kicked out six weeks before graduation. There was the younger Craig, the school's spiritual leader who years later de-converted and changed his name to Karma. There was Sabine, who met secretly with German boys. There was Mike who dated some of the school's most beautiful girls and later discovered he preferred boys. There was David, who ran around the dorm halls naked yelling "L'homme naturel!" and later became a Baptist missionary.

We missionary kids were no better and no worse than the best and worst missionaries. Here's to all the missionaries, the good ones and the bad ones! Here's to the many missionaries who nurtured us missionary kids, who took time away from saving souls to help us with ours! And here's to the bad apples, at least those we found out about! To the missionary who peeped at showering girls! To the missionary who beat up boys! To the missionary man who dared to sleep with men! Here's to all you missionaries and to all you missionary kids, the good ones, the bad ones, and those in between! I love you all. I am your son and your brother, no better than the worst of you.

"**W**hat man among you," says Christ in the famous parable, "if he has a hundred sheep and has lost one of them, does not leave the ninety-nine in the open pastures and go after the one which is lost, until he finds it?" Walking around the boy's dormitory after my parents left that September afternoon, I must have looked like a lost sheep, because one of the older boys decided to call me "Little Lamb."

The nickname stuck, and for the remaining four years I was called "Little Lamb."

I am leading you Believers on with my sanctimonious Bible quotation about sheep, because I was far from an innocent little lamb. In fact, my obsession about girls had not stopped just because I'd left French school; it was getting worse. In a self-portrait at the time, I inflated my skinny chest and arms so as to look as manly as possible. But my eyes, I made as sheep-like as I  could. And on my belt, I put my official nickname: "Little Lamb."

Me, I was a little lamb on the prowl. I wanted to be like my old French friend Daniel Martin. I wanted a girlfriend.

Dating at a missionary-kid boarding school was a tricky thing, however.

"We don't allow holding hands," one of our teachers explained to us, "because you never know where the arm stops."

My first attempt at going out with a girl did not go well. It lasted a week-end during which we never saw each other. She broke up with me in a note.

"John," it began. (Not even "Dear John.")

"I really can't go out with you," she continued.

"Please understand," she concluded, "Lov', MJ." She didn't even sign her full name.

Thankfully, to help me with my relationship woes, I had a trusted friend. I had met this friend in art class taught by Mr. Trowbridge. Unlike most of our Canadian Mennonite teachers, the very English Mr. Trowbridge exercised no discipline, and so most of art class was spent exchanging notes with my friend.

My friend understood my problems because she herself, a beautiful girl who was two years older than me, had already gone out with several boys. Her name was Dottie.

Dorothy, or Dottie as we all called her, the daughter of American missionaries in Germany, had gone out with several of the school's best-looking boys, each one of them older than me. Dottie was out of my league, and I knew it.

Needless to say, I was in love with Dottie. Even now, when my nose recalls the perfume she used to wear in Mr. Trowbridge's art class, I get goosebumps. There was no way I was ever going to be Dottie's boyfriend.

I settled with being Dottie's friend. Since I was a harmless ninth-grader, from time to time Dottie would come listen to me play the piano. She'd even sit next to me and ask me to play one of her favorite songs, like Queen's "Somebody to Love." I didn't sing at the time. I just played. I played my little heart out.

With the change from French school to missionary kid school, my main artistic outlet switched from drawing to music. At the Black Forest Academy, I graduated from French shlock to real rock 'n' roll music. The older boys initiated us into rock 'n' roll, and in exchange we young ones taught them a thing or two. By the end of  my ninth grade, I had developed a reputation for writing songs. I would sit at the piano and play my latest composition, and the older boys would listen.

Several of us decided to form a rock band. It wasn't easy having a rock band in a missionary kid boarding school. After our band performed using falsetto in church one Sunday, the principal Mr. Toews ordered me into his office.

"When you sing falsetto, you sound like a girl," Mr. Toews explained, "and that's not something a good Christian boy wants to do."

I walked out of Mr. Toews's office with my tail between my legs.

"When we both are far from this school," wrote a friend in the aftermath of the falsetto fiasco, "we will walk into a studio and record some rock 'n' roll music and send it to Mr. Toews!"

Our falsetto problem aside, my missionary kid rock band did have a very Christian name: The Grand Awakening.

We also had the good fortune to play from time to time in the studio of another Christian band, also made up of missionary kids. Except, unlike us, this band had an international hit. The band was called Deliverance.

Around the Black Forest Academy, Deliverance was legendary. Originally the gospel singers of the mission that had founded the Black Forest Academy, Deliverance edged towards a rock sound in the late 1970s, culminating in *Tightrope* (1979), which landed the band a minor hit, the ballad "Leaving L.A."

Lowly missionary kids who had made it big as rock 'n' rollers in the heart of pagan Europe – impressive!

The closest that my band the Grand Awakening ever got to being like Deliverance was using their practice studio in a forsaken hamlet outside of

Lörrach, a half-hour's bike ride from the boy's dormitory. We boys would set ourselves up in the studio still shimmering from Deliverance's aura, with Doug on the drums, the other Doug on vocals, Clark on guitar, Mark on bass and me at the Fender Rhoades, like we were rock gods. At the end of the day, tired but exhilarated, we'd ride back to the dorm, our guitars strapped to our backs, sweating the happy sweat of a satisfied dream that, at least for one day, we'd been as good as any rock god could ever dream of being.

Yes, the Black Forest Academy was changing me!

I started getting bolder with Dottie, in the hopes that she would consider me as her boyfriend, now that I was a bona fide missionary kid rock 'n' roll star.

"I hope we'll stay good friends next year, and that our relationship will grow into a better one," I wrote her at the end of that schoolyear.

That fall, after I had turned fifteen, Dottie, now a splendid seventeen years of age with gorgeous eyes, long brown hair, ruby lips, and I'd better stop there, noticed a difference in her Little Lamb.

"You've changed from last year, you know that?" she exclaimed.

Was it possible? Would she consider being my girlfriend?

Little by little, over the course of that fall, it just happened. I fell in love, she fell in love, we fell in love. There was nothing to it. Glances turned to stares, touches became strokes, and what little gap remained between us was closed with the holding of hands.

"You're all the good things I've known with anybody," I told her back then. "You're my best friend."

Those of you who have been reading this book from the beginning remember what I said earlier about my parents' courting, that all of us at some point or the other have said some very foolish things back when we were young and in love.

Well, so did Dottie and I. And when our declarations of love finally came, they gushed forth like icky Harlequin dialogue.

"You really are the only one that understands me and loves me," she wrote me in a note.

"Nothing will stop me from loving you," I wrote back, "nothing!"

With Dottie, I had found my partner. I was then, and I remain to this day, the object of a devotion so ferocious and constant that I believe no one in the world has ever been better loved than me. No words can describe it. And so, I will not attempt to.

That, dear readers, Believers, Unbelievers and Innocent Ones, is how, in the spring of 1980, I became Dottie's boyfriend and she my girlfriend. It seemed to us then that we were as good as married.

I was a teenager and I had everything. A beautiful girl to love and to confide in, a rock 'n' roll band to play my songs, and best of all, a home. What better home for an uprooted missionary kid than a boarding school full of uprooted missionary kids?

That spring of 1980, the Grand Awakening recorded its first cassette album in the little Deliverance studio on the road to Lörrach, sweating all day over the beautiful Fender Rhoades and the Ludwig drums.

It even sounded a little like Deliverance's *Tightrope*.

Now, I have been trying to explain to you about missionary kids in this book, but I'm afraid I haven't been doing a very good job. Some of you Believers may feel as if I have made things overly sad. Maybe they're too rosy for you Unbelievers. Some of you Innocent Readers may still be wondering, what exactly *is* a missionary kid?

Let's try something different. You Believers will like this idea, since it sounds biblical.

Being a missionary kid was like being on a ship, the Good Ship Missionary.

We missionary kids may have trembled at the storms of moving around, we may have shivered in the rains of our goodbyes, but one thing we knew. The Good Ship Missionary was going to get us safely to our ultimate destination, America. And we knew that, once we got to America, the storms of goodbyes and financial uncertainties would cease, because America was the land of milk and honey.

What we didn't know back then was that it was going to be difficult once we made it to America to return to Europe, given our parents' penniless vocation. No Prayer Letter or missionary slide show was ever going to be able to raise enough money to solve the intercontinental dilemma that was the missionary kid.

What we also didn't know, as missionary kids who had spent our entire childhood and adolescence sailing with our parents on the Good Ship Missionary, was that we were going to be set adrift in an ocean as vast and mysterious as God Himself.

The class of 1980, to which some of my band's members belonged, was the first to take the plunge. They left us all forlorn.

When, the next year, one or two came back to visit, something unspeakable had passed over them. But they pretended as if nothing was wrong.

Then came the year Dottie graduated. Every week we stared each other's eyes out on the bus to and from school, each hoping that an imprint of the one's face would etch itself on the other's mind as a safeguard, as a living photograph to be fondled during the long year apart.

That year, I was her Little Lamb and she was my Mary. So famously inseparable had we become at the Black Forest Academy that on Valentine's Day, months before our parting, we dressed up as the two characters, she as Mary and me as her lamb. I tried to be  brave, but I knew that, like the lost sheep in Jesus' story, I would soon be cursed to wander without my Mary. Then came the awful moment. We cried. Then we cried some more. And then we couldn't cry any longer. At the thought of her silent tear-stained cheeks on that last night, I still get a lump in my throat.

Unexpectedly, a few months later, I was able to visit Dottie in Frankfurt, days before her departure for the States, but it just made things worse. As if prolonging the agony, after our few days together, I missed the morning train.

We wandered the woods until the next train in the late afternoon. Through my tears as the train moved away, she faded from view, arrayed in a beautiful blue dress, mascara streaming down her beautiful young cheeks.

It was the worst goodbye of my life. I did not know if I would ever see my Dottie again.

The last year at the Black Forest Academy was one long winter day of waiting. Dottie and I wrote all the time. Today in our home those letters take up  several boxes, and I will spare you the mawkish prose, except for a note my love wrote me a year before our parting, eons earlier: "Ich habe Dich wirklich unheimlich lieb! Vergiß das bitte nicht!", which in English means, "I love you so, so much! Please never forget this!" Oh, my sweet angelic Marlene Dietrich, my beloved Mary, how I missed you that year, you will never know! Alone I visited all of our haunts, like this fountain that I drew, and I knew that I would die if at the end of it I did not find your smiling face.

Finally, it came, the moment when I too had to leave the cocoon of missionary kid school.

The graduation ceremony droned on like a long, slow-motion journey out of my past. My infancy in Morocco. My childhood in Marseille. My early adolescence in Grenoble. My teenage years in Germany. And the cumulative sounds and smells of each place, from the humming cicadas of the Mediterranean to the mossy womb of the Black Forest.

Finally, the time had come for me to bid one more infernal farewell. All of these places I now left behind as I sprang off the plank, diving off the Good Ship Missionary into the waters of the unknown.

I could not have seen it for concentrating on the plunge, but, if I had looked up at that moment, I would have seen dark clouds all across the ocean's horizon. Dark clouds creeping in, steady and sure.

A storm was coming.

Its name was America.

CHAPTER 7
AMERICA

Back when I was a kid in Marseille, Dad would tell us stories about the possum. The possum was a creature that lived in the wilds of America, where my Dad was raised. It crawled through the swamps and fed on snakes. So fierce was the possum that it could kill and devour an entire snake in a single bite. Dad even told us that, as a young man in Virginia, he had once captured a possum, and we

knew this was true because he had a picture to show for it, a picture of himself holding a possum captive on a leash.

But the legend of the possum was no match for an even more legendary story that Dad told us, about another indigenous American animal. I am speaking of the One-eyed Finkelfuss.

"Let me tell you the story of the One-eyed Finkelfuss," Dad would begin.

Then he would launch into his story, illustrating it with drawings of the One-eyed Finkelfuss, none of which survive today.

It is impossible for me to do justice to Dad's pictures of the One-eyed Finkelfuss, but, as the legend of the One-eyed Finkelfuss will vanish for all time if I do not attempt something, I will do what I can. Here is my recollection – mediocre, I know – of the One-eyed Finkelfuss.

Raised as an American far from America, I imagined America to be as fantastic as the One-eyed Finkelfuss. And that was still pretty much where things stood when I graduated from missionary kid boarding school and emigrated to the United States of America, which I believed to be the Land of Milk and Honey.

I was born in Morocco where I spent the first five years of my life, but I am not Moroccan. I was raised in France, can speak and write French fluently, and have even written scholarly articles and a book in French, yet I am not French. For four years I lived in Germany, but I am not German either. My maternal grandparents were Canadian, my high school degree is from a Canadian school (in Germany), I have lived longer in Canada than I have anywhere else in the world. But I know that I am not truly Canadian.

I, dear readers – Believer, Unbeliever and Innocent One – am just a missionary kid. An American missionary kid, to be exact. See how proud I look in the photograph on my Certificate of Citizenship? I was only five at the time, but already I knew, as the eldest son of American citizens, that I was officially a son of the American Empire, the greatest country in the world.

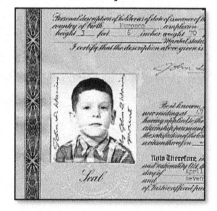

Every three years our family came to America, and we would tour the churches that supported us. We missionary kids were the stars of the show, exhibit A of our parents' spiritual ardor.

"Welcome Haines!" read the sign at the entrance of one church. (They hadn't figured out that the plural of Haines is Haineses.)

I was a famous missionary kid in America!

And yet, for all of this I am not truly American.

You see, missionary kids lack one thing, a thing that most other people have, whether they like it or not. What the missionary kid is missing is a home. At this point, I see you Believers and Unbelievers squirming, but please be patient for the sake of your weaker brothers and sisters the Innocent Ones.

Mainly what you Innocent Readers need to know is that, beginning around 1970, a few learned academics, incidentally all of them Americans and none of them missionary kids, wrote the first doctoral dissertations on missionary kids.

"Re-entry Experiences and Identity Formation of Third Culture Experienced Dependent Youth," went the title of one of these. "Third culture!" As if we came from some a secret Hogwarts located in between our land of birth and that of our parents!

No, what has defined us American missionary kids is not some mythical third country.

It is the *lack* of a country.

We American missionary kids may be sons and daughters of the American Empire. We may have felt, from time to time, a shiver of excitement at the sight of the imperial flag waving in the wind. We may have travelled to the furthest fringes of the world thanks to supporters working in the empire.

But the empire is not our home.

Dottie and I had agreed to meet outside a McDonalds in Pennsylvania, but we ended up meeting under a tree. After a year apart, Dottie in Minnesota and me in the Black Forest, I had made my way to America. At last we would see each other again. As our meeting point we had picked a McDonalds, out of nostalgia for the McDonalds in Basel from boarding school days.

Maybe to give herself a way out at the last minute, or maybe just as a joke, Dottie hid a way off under a tree. She hid and watched me approach the McDonalds. I looked around, wondered, and began despairing. And then I saw her standing there.

She was wearing the same dress as when I last saw her fading from my tear streaked eyes. It was perfect. It was as if we'd never been apart. That summer we took a bus west to Chicago to meet up  with the gang from Black Forest Academy days for a missionary kid wedding. Even my old band, The Grand Awakening, got back together for a day. We had all moved to America, but America was unreal. America was what it had always been, just another pitstop. Dottie and I were as happy as Adam and Eve in the garden.

One of the authors I mentioned earlier had the following to say about missionary kids: "The average IQ score of missionary kids runs between fifteen and twenty points above the general public in the United States."

Now, I don't know how he got that statistic, because no missionary I ever knew had enough spare change to give any of his kids an IQ test.

The other problem is that, whether or not we had an IQ higher than average was of little help to us, because the career options available for our outstanding IQs were, let's say, limited.

You Disenchanted Missionary Kid Unbelievers know exactly what I mean, but I am trying to explain things to the rest of you, and especially to you Innocent Ones who likely cannot imagine just how unimaginative things were in the career-counseling department for missionary kids some forty years ago.

So, let me lay it out as straightforwardly as possible.

Born in North Africa and raised in Europe, I could have majored in International Relations at, say, The University of Pennsylvania, in the city of Philadelphia where our mission headquarters were located. Unfortunately, most of my high school teachers had gone to Bible School. They considered any secular school off limits for us missionary kids. So, becoming an International Relations major at The University of Pennsylvania was out.

As a cosmopolitan artist, I could have majored in Engineering at Virginia Tech like my father or, better yet, in Art at Cambridge University like my teacher Mr. Trowbridge. Unfortunately, my father had dropped out of engineering to go to Bible College and Mr. Trowbridge never shared with us lowly missionary kids how he managed to get into Cambridge.

So, Cambridge and Virginia Tech were out.

In the end, we missionary kids were left with the only career in the world, in the opinion of our parents: missionary-hood. And the best way to prepare for missionary-hood was Christian college. And the best kind of Christian College was Bible College.

Then there was the financial advice.

"You could always tutor in French for extra money or sell some of your art work," my mother explained to me during my first few months in America.

"Necessity is the mother of invention," she continued.

"We're going by suggestions from another missionary kid who has spent a year or two in the States," she added, in an attempt to make things better.

It didn't, because going to missionary kids for financial advice is generally not a good idea, especially since some of the missionary kids to whom my mother was talking had some pretty outdated advice.

"I was talking to a sixty-year old missionary kid," she wrote at the beginning of the same letter. "He was so full of stories! His very first memory was returning on furlough with his parents by freight at age three while visiting China."

All of that to say that Dottie and I did what we missionary kids were expected to do and what nearly all of our boarding-school classmates did. After the Black Forest Academy, we went to a Christian school.

That fall, Dottie attended what is perhaps the most obscure and insular of all Bible schools in America, Lancaster Bible College.

As for me, in the fall of 1982, I started my freshman year in a pretty Christian sounding school.

It was called Messiah College. Messiah, for short.

When William F. Buckley, while still an undergraduate student at Yale University, wrote the immature diatribe against his professors that became the neoconservative manifesto, *God and Man at Yale*, he made one basic mistake.

William F. Buckley made the mistake of being born at the wrong time.

Most American colleges, no matter how religious at the beginning – and they were usually very religious – have eventually become considerably less so over time.

William F. Buckley's school of choice in the 1940s, the very prestigious Yale University, had once been the Collegiate School for the training of Congregationalist ministers. These ministers had founded Yale after leaving Harvard, which they considered too liberal. Harvard, the oldest and most prestigious of them all, had been founded as a boot camp for Puritan preachers.

By the 1940s, however, Yale had long strayed from its godly roots. For a God-hankering academic like William F. Buckley, Yale was a very poor choice!

No, to satisfy his craving for religion in 1945, the twenty-year old William F. Buckley should have looked elsewhere.

As it happens, there were a good number of very religious colleges available to the likes of William F. Buckley at the time.

Founded only a few decades earlier, Columbia Bible College (which my parents attended) would have dished up plenty of God along with its man for the future author of *God and Man at Yale*.

Or, if he'd been a real spiritual diehard, William F. Buckley might have escaped to the plains of Canada and attended Briarcrest Bible Institute, a young and vibrant place.

And, as a proud graduate of either Columbia Bible College or Briarcrest Bible Institute, given William F. Buckley's longevity, he would have eventually been able to accuse his alma mater of irreligion.

By the late 1980s, with growing enrollment and new graduate programs, Columbia Bible College and Briarcrest Bible Institute had dropped the word "Bible" from their names.

No more Bible College and Bible Institute. They were now called "Columbia International University" and "Briarcrest College."

Living on the evangelical reservation of the Black Forest Academy, most of us missionary kids assumed our university options were limited to the Bible Institutes and Christian Colleges advertised in the back of our yearbooks. Columbia Bible College, my parents'

and sister's alma mater, was regularly featured in the Black Forest Academy yearbook.

We missionary kids didn't know about first tier, second tier, or third tier schools. For all we knew, America had only two tiers: Bible School and Christian College.

I attended Messiah College mainly because it was the only option available, and because one or two other kids from our mission had gone there.

Problem was, Messiah College was missionary kid school all over again!

There was enforced chapel duty and sexual abstinence by vigilant resident assistants on each floor of our dorms. At Messiah, we took our rock 'n' roll without the drugs, our English lit without Portnoy's repulsive habit, our American history without Betty Friedan's whining, and our drawing classes without nude models.

If I had been mildly motivated in French school and at the Black Forest Academy, at Messiah I became downright apathetic.

All I wanted to do was sing rock 'n' roll and make it big in the Land of Milk and Honey. My new band's name was Inner Mission, a good choice for a missionary kid's band. We didn't drink or do drugs.

But our lead guitarist, a preacher's kid by the name of Darrell, sure played like he did. Darrell slept during the day and roamed at night when all of God's wild creatures come out to play. We never knew where Darrell had been the night before, but whatever it was, it made for some pretty inspiring guitar playing. I enjoyed our band very much, and I like to think that, if I'd stuck around long enough at Messiah, we would have made a hit record.

Who knows?

I never found out, because the old urge to move on was kicking in something fierce.

For most of us missionary kids, those first few years in America were rough. Take my old boarding school roommate Stan. No sooner had he left the Black Forest Academy than Stan went on a spree of drinking and sleeping with girls that didn't stop until years later.

Another classmate of mine, David, started taking valium. "I had no direction, no joy," David wrote me: "it was excruciating depression."

A few years into our American migration, it was becoming clear to most of us missionary kids that America was not the Land of Milk and Honey.

By the second year at Messiah, all I wanted was to leave. I had had enough! I wanted to get out of Christian places and into the real Land of Milk and Honey – wherever that was – and make some money. I wanted to paint fabulous art. I wanted to be a rock 'n' roll star in America.

But first, I wanted to get married.

To illustrate for you how I felt then, I would like to invoke my dog Tessa, whom you may remember. From time to time, Tessa will get the heebie-jeebies. And when Tessa gets the heebie-jeebies, she runs. And when Tessa runs, she runs very, very fast.

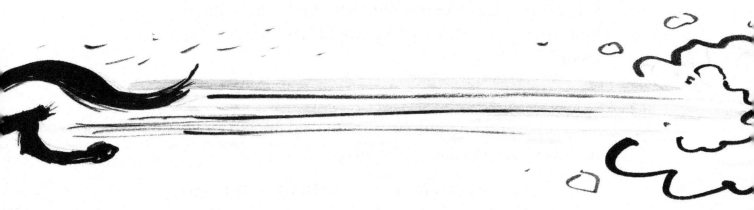

I have tried to draw for you Tessa running with the heebie-jeebies, but all I managed was this. You get the point, though. When the heebie-jeebies hit Tessa, there's no accounting for how fast she will run.

The next year, my second and last year at Messiah College, just flew by.

I took mostly art classes, but my heart wasn't in it.

I whipped Inner Mission into shape for one last concert where I wore my cool black-and-white striped pants that a friend had brought me from Germany. I took on two part-time jobs to make ends meet.

On one of the last weeks of school, me and a classmate of mine from the art program took one of my 3-D art projects, a wire-and-plaster monstrosity we had nicknamed Igor, and threw it over a covered bridge into the Yellow Breeches Creek. At first, Igor sank. Then he wobbled back up to the surface. After a while, he took his leave, limping downstream. Who  knows what became of Igor? I couldn't have cared less. At last, like Igor, I was floating away. I was moving on.

Finally, I was leaving Christian College and going off to make my fortune in the secular Land of Milk and Honey with the only friend I had left in the world, Dottie, a missionary kid.

CHAPTER 8
SPEAKING IN TONGUES

I am afraid I now have something sad to tell you about my dog Tessa, so please brace yourselves. Not too long ago, I discovered that Tessa has Pannus, an eye disease specific to German Shepherds. Unless Tessa has daily eye drops she will go blind from her  Pannus. So now, three times a day, I put drops into both of her eyes. And every day, Tessa does what she has to do.

"Tessa!" I call out, "let's do your drops."

Tessa comes running, because she knows that she has to have her drops.

"Give me a sit."

Tessa sits. Her ears go back. Her eyes squint as the bottle approaches. Her toes curl as each drop goes in. After the last drop, Tessa waits, because there's one more thing left in our routine.

"All done," I whisper and put the bottle away. Tessa sighs a dog-sigh. I lean back down, stroke her neck, pull in close, and she licks my nose.

The point of this story is that we all do what we must to survive.

In the fall of 1984, newly married in the Land of Milk and Honey, I did what I had to do. I went back into the Christian furnace, like Daniel in the lions' den. For two full years, I worked as a telemarketer for the Christian Broadcasting Network in Virginia Beach, Virginia.

The choice of Virginia had been arbitrary. Dottie's parents had recently moved there; it was neither their home nor ours, but we all went anyway.

Hear now, patient readers, of the fourth happy Twist of Fate in my story, for moving to Virginia allowed me, for the first and only time in my life, to see one of my grandparents on a regular basis.

As Fate would have it, he was the best one of the lot.

Grampy Haines, as Joy and I called him, was a man easily mythologized. As far as I knew, there  walked on God's earth no greater man than Grampy Haines. Unlike my Dad, Grampy was no evangelical. No, for Grampy, religion was just another civic duty, right up there with going to the Masonic Lodge and the bowling club. My favorite picture of Grampy shows him leaning forward as he propels the ball down the bowling alley.

I soon learned that Grampy indulged in hell-bound heathen activities such as smoking and drinking. And so, for most of my childhood and adolescence, I assumed that, sadly, Grampy would have to go to hell.

At some point, shortly before he died, Grampy's status miraculously changed, although he hadn't become born again. I was never quite sure how or when the change happened, but I was glad to know that, after all, Grampy was going to heaven rather than to hell.

‿◞

Grampy was one of those present when Dottie and I got married in Norfolk, Virginia. It was a small ceremony with a low-cost reception afterwards. Missionary-kid style.

We barely got a place to live in time for the wedding. After scouring the papers for months, we found a rental we could afford.

"Wow, this sounds great," I told Dottie. "Let's check it out right away!"

When we got there, we discovered that everyone except for us was black and that there was no electricity or running water. The house we eventually wound up renting was in a white neighborhood. But one block down, across an invisible but very definite line, was the poor black section.

After a modest honeymoon, Dottie and I moved in to our cheap apartment. In that first year of marriage, we had nothing except the one thing that mattered, each other. Only six years earlier, we had started out as friends in the Black Forest. Now newly married, we had nothing in  America but each other, and so we devoted ourselves to the sweet labor of loving each other.

Desperate for work, I responded to an ad that looked promising.

"Look honey," I told my young wife, "here's a job at the Christian Broadcasting Network!"

I didn't know what the Christian Broadcasting Network was, but my being a missionary kid was bound to be an asset in a place with a name like that. I filled out the questions on the application form.

"Are you a Christian?" Yes!

"Do you have experience praying?" Yes!

"Have you received the Baptism of the Holy Spirit?"

I'd never heard that expression before, but I figured if anyone had ever received the Baptism of the Holy Spirit, it would be a missionary kid.

I know, I know, Innocent Ones. You need an explanation here, so let me, as quickly as possible, explain to you about the Baptism of the Holy Spirit. You Believers and Unbelievers just hold your tongues and sit tight.

You see, Innocent Readers, my parents looked down on their parents and many other Christians besides for not being born again. But there existed Christians who looked down on my parents, if you can believe it! These Christians believed in an extra step after being born again, and this was the Baptism of the Holy Spirit.

I was never quite clear on exactly what the Baptism of the Holy Spirit was, except for one thing. You had to practice what was called speaking in tongues. So far as I could tell, speaking in tongues involved closing your eyes, raising your hands, and improvising on a series of Arabic sounding syllables.

"Shandalah baseekah!"

I even tried it myself once or twice.

"Shandalah baseekah," I burst out, raising my hands as high as I dared.

To be honest with you, I was never very good at speaking in tongues, but I was certainly willing to learn as I explained to them when they interviewed me at the Christian Broadcasting Network, and that must have been good enough because, next thing I knew, I was working full time as a telemarketer for the Christian Broadcasting Network in Virginia Beach, Virginia, at the rate of $4.75 an hour with health benefits.

When I started working for the Christian Broadcasting Network, the company was in full expansion mode thanks to its many donors. Most of these donors had contacted the network during one of its live-broadcast telethons.

What few people knew at the time was that the successful running of the Christian Broadcasting Network owed to a hundred telemarketers working in the windowless bowels of the network. These telemarketers made over eight thousand calls all across America every day.

We telemarketers would settle into our cubicles and get hooked up by a headset to an automatic-dialing machine that spewed out phone numbers. Facing us was a binder with a script, as you can see at the right hand of the fellow telemarketer I drew one day at work. Six days a week, every week of the year, we telemarketers called people who had innocently contacted the Christian Broadcasting Network during one of its telethons.

"Hello?" Mildred would say, answering the phone.

"Hello, Mildred," I would say, "this is John with the 700 Club. (The "700 Club" was the name of the Christian Broadcasting Network's flagship show.)

"How are you today, Mildred?"

"Pat? Pat? Is it you, Pat?"

"No, Mildred, this is John with the 700 Club, but I do have a message for you from Pat Robertson. Would you like to hear it?"

"Oh, yes, Pat! Pat, I was wondering—"

"Here, you go Ma'am." I would press the return key and Mildred was off, rambling away to Pat as his cassette-recorded message ran for exactly one minute and sixteen seconds. Meanwhile, the automatic-dialing machine kept on dialing, and I would take a few more calls.

"Hello, again Mildred," I would say after the message was finished, interrupting Mildred's conversation with Pat's recorded ghost.

"—was exactly what I was telling my friend Diane just yesterday—"

"Mildred, this is John. I hope you enjoyed Pat's message."

Pause.

"Pat?"

"We're done with Pat's message, now, Mildred, but I can pray for you if you like," I would continue, anxiously eyeing my script. The clock was ticking.

"What one thing would you like to pray about today, Mildred?" I would emphasize the word "one."

What Mildred did not know was that I had no more than four minutes to listen to her request, pray, and move on to the money pitch. Mildred would tell me her ailment of the moment, and I would pray as efficiently and heartily as possible.

"Amen, and amen," I would conclude, mimicking Pat's style as best I could.

"Shandalah, shandalah," Mildred would murmur, still under the spell of the magical moment she and Pat were sharing.

"And shandalah baseekah to you, Mildred! Now, Mildred," I would continue, following my script, "as you heard Pat say, CBN needs your help today with our brand-new building project. Would you like to give a one-time gift towards this project?"

"Well, I don't know, Pat," Mildred would say, "I already give $25 a month to the 700 Club, and I don't have much money..."

"Just a one-time gift, today, Mildred?"

"Well, I suppose I could give $100."

"A hundred dollars, that's great, Mildred, that's great," I would say, typing into the computer the correct dollar amount next to Mildred's information.

"All right," I would say. "God bless you, Mildred."

"God bless you too, Pat."

During the two years that I worked at the Christian Broadcasting Network, I learned a lot. For starters, I learned that, even though I was a missionary kid, I had to work like everyone else. I learned that if your only option for income is to sit at a computer terminal chained to an automatic-dialing machine along with dozens of other  telemarketers, then that is what you will do. Just like my dog Tessa with her eye-drops.

Few people in the Christian Broadcasting Network's telemarketing department lasted longer than six months. I worked there for two years.

Not only did I learn about needing to work, I also learned about African-Americans. Of those working in the telemarketing department, most were in the same pecuniary pickle as myself. Some were graduate students in the Christian Broadcasting Network's Regent University, but many were black folks commuting in from all around the Chesapeake Bay. The word "Negro" had not been used in Virginia for roughly twenty years, depending on where you lived, but most of the African Americans who worked alongside me had a life much further removed from the American dream than even this poor missionary kid.

I also learned that there were two ways to do the speaking in tongues. The white way and the black way.

Most white people like myself did the speaking in tongues with restraint. We would begin with a polite "Shandalah baseekah," and quickly retreat into some muttered English. The white man's skill at tongues is so mediocre that, as the story goes, Pat Robertson, the head of the Christian Broadcasting Network, had learned his tongues at the feet of a Korean lady nicknamed "the tongues woman."

Nobody, however, does the speaking in tongues like a black woman.

When one of my black female colleagues in the telemarketing department would stand up in our daily chapel meetings to do the speaking in tongues, those sitting next to her would slide their chairs away an inch or two.

Then she would start the tongues, her head bowed low, her arms floating up.

Pretty soon the tongues would seize her whole body, shaking it like a Raggedy Ann doll until she was pouring out a torrent of tongues, her mouth like the spout of a pressure-filled balloon doing its best to release the Holy Ghost as fast as possible, leaving the white man's measly "Shandalah baseekah" in the dust.

Black tongues make white tongues look like an English lord's burp after a pleasant meal.

Me, a missionary kid born in Africa, I always assumed the difference was on account of the suppressed energy from African Americans' enslavement for hundreds of years. My good friend William, pictured here, once tried to explain to me the difference between the religion of white and black Americans. At some point, since I just wasn't getting it,  William started speaking in parables, which if you think about it is kind of like speaking in tongues.

"The white man," said William, "goes to church." Here he exaggerated the white "r."

"But the black man goes to chu'ch." No "r."

"Whites are sanctified," William continued. "But blacks are san'ified." William performed the glottal stop in the middle of this word more like a glottal heave: "san-'AH-fied!"

It was then I realised that I would never understand the ways of the black man, who was apparently even more of a stranger in America than the missionary kid.

Years after my time in Virginia, I would learn that my Grampy Haines had once been poor like me. This was during the Great Depression. For most of the 1930s, Grampy had moved from job to job, struggling to keep his fledgling family clothed and fed.

During our two years in Virginia, Dottie and I saw Grampy often enough for me to really start feeling like his grandson – his only grandson. After our old Chrysler gave up the ghost, Grampy lent us five thousand dollars for the purchase of another car, and we bought a nearly new Toyota. Here I am  with my Grampy, standing next to the precious Toyota. Maybe I was disillusioned by America by then, but at least Grampy was by my side.

After two years in Virginia, despite Dottie and I working full-time, we had nothing to show except for a financial debt that hadn't been there when we first started working.

Slowly it was sinking in that America was not the Land of Milk and Honey.

So, we decided to do the only logical thing for two newly married missionary kids. We decided to go back onboard the Good Ship Missionary whence we'd come. And to accomplish this, we set off for the place where both of our parents had started.

Bible School.

I wrote to all of the friends and relatives I could think of and announced our decision to go to Bible School. I was writing my very own Prayer Letter!

"Dottie and I have recently felt called of God to full-time Christian service," I stated, slipping right into missionary jargon, as natural to me as high-minded quibbling to a professor's child.

My parents were beaming. With both Joy and me in Bible College that year, they could not have been prouder of their two missionary kids!

Like the Children of Israel packing up their tents and leaving the desert for the Promised Land, Dottie and I said goodbye to Virginia and to my grandfather.

Like two missionaries, we were moving on.

We were going to a place I had never seen before in my life, a place called Bemidji.

CHAPTER 9
SOCRATES

If you're making your way to Bemidji, Minnesota, likely you'll be coming from the south. Less likely from the north. Either way, you'll find yourself in the land where, long before Christianity existed, the Dakota buried their dead in mounds that still lie like sleeping giants on the plains.

If you do come from the north, you'll arrive the same way the Ojibway did, shoved into Dakota territory by my ancestors the Christians. The Ojibway decided to cooperate with the Christians, but all they got for their cooperation was a remote corner of the vast land they had once roamed with the Dakota.

In which remote corner Bemidji is located.

But, like I say, you'll probably be coming to Bemidji from the south. If you arrive by boat, you'll row up the Mississippi through Prairie du Chien, where in 1825 the Christians told the Dakota where they could and could not go. Paddling upstream you'll come to Saint Paul, where missionaries tried their hand at converting the Dakota whom they called "reckless sons of Belial."

On your way, you'll see in the distance Traverse des Sioux, where in 1851 the Dakota sold all their land to Christians at the bargain price of three cents an acre. And just south of this, the city of Mankato, where a little later the troubles with the Dakota were concluded with the hanging of thirty-eight warriors.

Continuing up the Mississippi, you'll float through Brainerd and leave the fields behind. Deeper and deeper into north-country you'll go, through Sandy Lake where began the exodus of the Ojibway, and across Lake Winnibigoshish, not far from where took place the Battle of Leech Lake, the last Indian uprising in America.

And then, heading straight for White Earth where the Ojibway still live, you'll follow the Mississippi River into Lake Bemidji. Bemidji, from "bemijigamaag." This means, "lake that goes through another body of water."

Like I say, that's assuming you want to go to Bemidji, Minnesota.

When, at the age of twenty-two, I drove into the north-country of Minnesota, I was bowled over. I had never experienced anything like it. This was the Wild West, the real America!

Everywhere were statues of Paul Bunyan, the wild man of America. Women may have existed in this wild west, but I couldn't find a single trace of them. There were only bearded northern men. Northern men who, just prior to felling trees had evidently felled the Indian, for there was no trace of him, either.

My neighbor Mike here in Ontario kind of reminds me of Paul Bunyan. Not too long ago, Mike and I decided to cut down a few trees.

"Let's go play Paul Bunyan," Mike said.

You should have seen Mike cut down trees with his chainsaw! I have never met Paul Bunyan, but without a doubt he must have resembled my neighbor Mike. Mike was wearing his snowmobile helmet and his protective pants, just in case the chainsaw accidentally slipped from his hands. You should have heard how the mighty  instrument roared in his manly hands! How the woodchips flew as Mike leaned into each log!

After several hours of doing this, Mike and I took a break and sat down to eat a sandwich.

"You know," Mike told me, "as a kid I went to Sunday School every week."

"Sunday School!" said I. "But, Mike, didn't you tell me earlier that you don't do religion?"

"That's right," Mike answered. "Now I don't. But as a kid I was made to attend church and Sunday School every week. After years of that," Mike concluded, "I wanted nothing to do with religion." I was speechless. How could someone as irreligious as my good neighbor Mike have come from religious stock?

Later I thought about it, and it made sense. It makes sense that those raised by heathens like my Dad convert to fundamentalism, and those raised by fundamentalists like Mike convert to heathenism.

Sometimes that's how it works. You've just got to change. It doesn't matter how or what to. You've just got to change.

And that, dear Innocent Ones, and you Believers and Unbelievers, is exactly what happened to me in Bemidji, Minnesota. A change came over me.

Like Virginia Beach, the choice of Bemidji as the next move for two young married missionary kids had been dictated by chance. A friend of Dottie's family had gone there years before, and so, for lack of a better plan, when Dottie and I had had enough of Virginia and figured that if anything in America was worth trying it was Bible College, we picked Oak Hills Bible College in Bemjidi.

Created as a backwoods substitute for Moody Bible Institute, the evangelical powerhouse in Chicago, Oak Hills offered a curriculum similar to Moody's, with a difference. In the spirit of the north-woods, there was something unregulated about the place.

For example, we had been raised to believe that once you made a confession of faith, you were going to heaven. Oak Hills put this belief to the test.

"One must slip over into a different way of looking at things," one teacher told us.

We had been taught that the Bible was the word of God. This too was questioned.

"We know almost nothing about what Christ's original words really were," said the same teacher.

What, Believers? Outrageous, you say? Not really. What my Bible teacher said wasn't as outrageous as all that. He was just teaching us how to ask questions. One by one, all of our received beliefs were inspected, and found wanting. This particular teacher was a master at the art of questioning. He did it in a most disarming way. It always began with a simple, "Yeah, but." Sitting in class, I took it all in, and at one point drew this cartoon of him.

That first year in Bemidji, I discovered the cold of the north-woods of Minnesota. For the first time in my life, I rode a snowmobile on top of a frozen lake.

I also stoked the school's main wood furnace. Every day, no matter how cold or snowy, I would start an old pickup truck, fill its battered bed with wood, then haul the wood and stack it for the next morning when, hours before dawn, I would heave the logs into the fireplace, light a match, and watch the bark and wood climax together into roaring flames.

Thus was I born again, a man of the north-woods.

My face even began to change. By the spring of that first year in Bemidji, less than a year after leaving  the monastic seclusion of the telemarketing booth in Virginia, my beard had grown to unprecedented fullness. Perhaps the extra dose of Bible readings was helping, making me not only into a man of the north-woods, but into a Biblical prophet as well.

Meanwhile, my teacher's instruction in questioning was beginning to take its toll. As my first year at Bible College wore on, I was having more and more doubts about becoming a missionary. I still wanted to be a rock 'n' roll star.

Around that time, one of my old bandmates from the Black Forest Academy wrote me from London, England, where he was living.

"Ever since we were at boarding school," Doug wrote, "you and I have talked about starting a band and having a career in music, but we've never acted on it. How about if you move to London and we give it a try?"

I was torn. Hadn't I come to Bible College to become a missionary?

"You must kill your musical dream," said the teacher I cited earlier. I had come to him for advice, and this was not what I wanted to hear.

"Kill your musical dream," he said, "like the red lizard in C.S. Lewis' *Great Divorce*."

I had never read *The Great Divorce*, and consequently had no idea what the red lizard was, but one thing I knew: if any authority was unassailable, it was C.S. Lewis. My mother adored C.S. Lewis. C.S. Lewis was right up there with Moses and Dr. Steele.

So, I decided to listen to C.S. Lewis. I killed my musical dream of becoming a rock 'n' roll star, just like the red lizard in *The Great Divorce*, and threw myself into my studies, at the feet of the greatest teacher I have ever known. This is the teacher whose words I have been citing in the last few pages. Thanks to this teacher, the fifth happy Twist of Fate in my story, I became genuinely curious for the first time in my life.

His name was Dean Fredrikson, and he was my Socrates.

"God has appointed me to this city," Socrates once told the citizens of Athens, "this city that is like a large, lazy horse requiring the stimulation of a stinging fly." Like a gift from God, Socrates declared, he would act as a fly, buzzing away until the horse was roused into action. In this famous passage from Plato's *Apology*, Socrates describes the ideal teacher, the one who goads the student into teaching himself.

Over my fifty some years, most of them spent in academia, I have listened to some pretty good teachers. I have heard the finest master of the Collège de France. I have sat enraptured by one of the best dons of Oxford. I have had dinner with some of the most prominent lights of Harvard University.

But none of these have come close to the man I met at an obscure Bible College tucked away in the north-woods, the man who would become my Socrates, Dean Fredrikson.

Dean Fredrikson had been a missionary in Portugal for twenty-five years. Bible Institute was the extent of Dean's formal education. The rest he had done himself. He had read A.W. Tozer and Oswald Chambers, like everyone else. But he had also read Plato, Descartes, Søren Kierkegaard and Margaret Mead – none on the reading list at the Prairie Bible Institute.

This unorthodox host distilled in Dean's head to form his own homebrewed doctrine. Dean Fredrikson may not have invented Christianity, but his version of it was unlike anything we students had ever encountered.

At Oak Hills, Dean had taught nearly everything, from the history of science to hermeneutics. Every class went pretty much the same way. Dean would amble into the room, still refreshed from skiing across the frozen lake or bow-hunting deer over the weekend. He would slouch into his chair and cock that  homely Socratic stump of a face. Then he would begin to ramble.

It was the rambling that did us in.

Half lecture, half sermon, Dean's meandering improvisations dismantled the things we took for granted, such as the literal interpretation of Scripture or the calling of God. None of this dogma interested him. Dean was after the spirit of the thing.

"What does it mean to be a Christian?" was all he wanted to know.

After hearing the question enough times, even us missionary kids were beginning to think that we didn't know what it meant to be a Christian after all.

"How do we know what a real Christian is?" a frustrated student asked Dean one day after hearing his rhetorical question one too many times.

Dean waited a beat.

"Is Roy *really* a Christian?" Dean burst out as he pointed to Roy, another student in the class.

Again, he waited a beat, just long enough to keep us wondering.

"How the Sam Hill do I know?"

That's as close as Dean Fredrikson ever came to swearing.

After sufficiently stirring the pot, Dean would wind down his rambling with a self-dismissive phrase.

"Buy it or sell it," he would say. Or, "OK, that's enough of that."

Then, after a pause, he would ask a question. Softly, deliberately. Then he would wait.

Slowly, we students would begin to talk.

In truth, the sole purpose of Dean's earlier rambling had been to bide time, time until the student mustered up the courage to sound his own mind. Slowly but surely, the student would begin rambling all on his own, and eventually he would pause to look around him. Only then would the student see that a change had taken place. For a brief time, but for a time at least, the student had become the teacher.

And there was the teacher, sitting and looking on, beaming that impish smile, pleased with his work. For the teacher's work was the student.

Dean Fredrikson was no apostate, although some students did wonder. No, Dean was a Christian to the core. But it mattered less to Dean what could be said about Christianity than what should be done about it. For Dean, it was the doing that counted. And to start doing, one had to start in the only place possible, the beginning and end of religion and of education alike.

One begins and ends with oneself.

Mostly, Dean made me curious – curious to read the many authors whose names he dropped in the course of his rambling. I had never enjoyed reading until then, but now I began to read. I read about worlds I never knew existed and then I read on about the worlds I already knew, or assumed I knew.

Dean made me insatiably curious about history.

The change I was undergoing at Bible School was obvious and traumatic for my parents. For one, they could see that I had abandoned the idea of being a missionary. Exactly what kind of Bible School was this, they wondered, that trained its students in doubt rather than belief?

Most worrisome was my new habit of questioning things. Probably at some point, Mom and Dad began to fear that all of this would end up sending me to hell.

Once or twice I tried to describe to them the new things I was learning, but this just made the situation worse.

I remember on two separate occasions arguing with Dad and then with Mom, explaining how my beliefs differed from theirs, that I was still a Christian but that I felt differently about things like the inerrancy of the Bible. They both cried. Neither knew what to say.

You see, Innocent Ones, we missionary kids are not accustomed to debating with our missionary parents the way academics do. All that debating produced was my Mom and Dad fearing for the fate of my soul.

They were terrified. And, to be perfectly honest, at times so was I.

Gradually, my parents and I began to avoid the topic of the Bible, in fact a whole chain of once shared beliefs whose absence now hung about in the room like a dead relative whom everyone forgets because it's just easier that way.

It was around this time that I stopped reading the Bible daily as I had done ever since I was a child. It was not that the Bible no longer interested me, just that there were so many other stories to read besides those in the Bible, to make sense of the Bible and of myself as its reader. The story of America, for example, which was proving to be bigger than I had ever imagined.

I was done with Bible school. My training as a missionary was over.

Once again, it was time to say goodbye.

But this time, I had no idea where I was going.

Like the Indian pictured on the state seal of Minnesota, which I have reproduced for you here in this drawing, I was riding off. I was bidding farewell

to the legends and lands of my missionary kid past and riding off into the unknown. The prospect was as frightening as it was thrilling. I had no way of knowing then that all of these undiscovered histories, the long ones and the short ones, those closest to me and those so remote from my experience that I had yet to know of their existence, that they all would lead me back to the one familiar place, to the place where the master gently leads the student by the hand.

Yes, yes, Believers.

This time you are right. I was losing my way.

But you know as well as I do that I needed to lose my way in order to find it again. That's just how it works sometimes.

Like my neighbor Mike, a man of the northwoods who reminds me a bit of Paul Bunyan, sometimes like Mike, you've got to change. Some have to change from apostate to evangelical, others from evangelical to apostate. And a few of us bounce back and forth between the two, not knowing where we'll end up.

But, like I said before, the how, when or where of it doesn't matter. That's just how it goes. You've got to move on and say goodbye.

CHAPTER 10
LADY ACADEME

And that's more or less how I ended up falling for Lady Academe. That and the fact that I started missing the places I'd said goodbye to over the years. By the time I quit Bible College, I had been away from Europe for six years. And, since I was a poor missionary kid stuck in the north-woods of Minnesota, it would be a while yet before I could go back. I missed my homelands terribly.

I was not the only one to feel this way.

One missionary kid I knew started working for an airline company which gave him free flights back to Germany. Another put a postcard of the lavender fields of Provence on her refrigerator, and she stared at that postcard until tears came to her eyes.

Me, I didn't even have a postcard to put on my refrigerator. So, out of desperation, I did the only thing I could do. I started reading French novels.

Now, I confess that I used to hate reading novels. There's too many words and too little action. Well, I couldn't have picked a worse French novel with which to begin! Stendhal's *Le rouge et le noir*, the story of an affair between a country bumpkin named Julien and the mayor's wife, Madame de Rênal.

That's it. For five hundred pages.

To make it through *Le rouge et le noir*, I tried picturing it as a movie. Here is how I imagined Julien, in a scene early in the book where he is engrossed in Napoleon's memoirs instead of the religious book he's supposed to be reading ...

SCENE 4   EXTERIOR - THE SAWMILL AT VERRIÈRES

WIDE SHOT - THE VALLEY

A shed by a river at the foot of the Jura Mountains. Birdsong, faintly.

CUT TO: LONG SHOT - SHED

A saw cuts wood pushed by a wheel that is turned by the river below. SLOW PAN UP from the saw to the rafters on which sits a young man. He reads, oblivious to the saw.

CUT TO: MEDIUM SHOT - JULIEN

We see his dark curly hair, his angelic face, and the book's title: *Mémorial de Saint-Hélène*, by Napoléon Bonaparte. Suddenly, off-screen left, a gruff voice:

> MR. SOREL
>
> Lazy boy! Still reading your damned books when you should be watching the saw?

"John!"

The Jura Mountains disappeared. The river and the birds stopped their gurgling and chirping.

"John," repeated the voice, "are you coming out of the bathroom?" It was the manager of the carpet store where I was working full-time for a year.

I had been reading *Le rouge et le noir* in the bathroom, the only place at work where I could be alone. After using a piece of toilet paper as a bookmark, I closed the book, finished my business and emerged from the bathroom, trying to hide the book in my hand.

"Is that what you're doing in there?" said the manager. "Reading a book? Do that on your break, not in the bathroom!"

How could the manager of the carpet store have understood how important Stendhal's *Le rouge et le noir* was? Not only was it transporting me back to France, this novel was preparing me to finally leave the Christian reservation where I'd been stuck all my life, including the carpet store which was run by a couple of charismatic Christians. I was about to leave all things Christian behind. I was going to Bemidji State University.

Dottie, who by now was using her given name, Dorothy, had been the first to make the leap from Bible College to a state university. I followed in her footsteps and started at Bemidji State as a double major in Music Education and French Literature. I basked in the intoxicating perfume of Lady Academe. I sang in choirs where I dressed up in pointy shoes and a feathered hat. I read every bit  of French literature I could get my hands on, from the Song of Roland to Albert Camus' *Stranger*.

As I did these things, my academic confidence increased. Like Julien with Madame de Rênal in *Le rouge et le noir*, I was falling under the spell of Lady Academe.

```
SCENE 6    INTERIOR   THE MAYOR'S MANSION

LONG SHOT of the hall of a great country house.
Madame de Rênal stands next to Julien who has just
been introduced as her children's tutor.  She is
worried about her children.

CUT TO: MEDIUM SHOT - JULIEN AND MADAME DE RÊNAL

Madame wears a summer dress covered by a shawl.
Julien wears a white shirt and holds a purple
jacket folded over his arm.  His black curly hair
is still wet from dipping it in the village
fountain on the way there.

                    JULIEN

     Never, Madame, will I hurt your children; I
     swear it before God!

Julien seizes Madame's hand and presses it to his
lips.  Her shawl slips down, revealing her bare
arm.  She flushes.  He releases her hand. Their
eyes meet.  They look away.
```

"John!"

It was the carpet store manager again.

I pulled out a piece of toilet paper, marked my place in the book, did what I had to do and walked out.

By then, I was only working part-time at the carpet store, and was taken up with full-time studies. Like Julien in the scene from *Le rouge et le noir*, my youthful missionary-kid hair still dripping from the fountain of evangelicalism, I had entered the mansion of Lady Academe, my Madame de Rênal.

"Daddy's a missionary," I had once complained to Mom back in Grenoble. "That's not a real job."

"Let's have devotions together," Mom said, opening up her Bible.

"First Timothy 3, verse 4: 'If a man wants to be a church overseer', which is basically a missionary, 'he must manage his household and keep his children under control'."

Mom looked up. "That, Johnny, is what your Daddy does."

That was probably when the first seeds of doubt were sewn about my ever becoming a missionary.

Once I started at Bemidji State University, it was settled. I was leaving the world of missionaries and missionary kids behind me! I was going to be a secular academic professor, even more splendid than Dr. Steele!

I would go to graduate school! To graduate school in England, no less!

One day, a don from Oxford visited Bemidji State University and suggested I apply for graduate studies in England. I applied, and to my complete surprise, received a letter back.

"You are being considered for our programme," the letter stated. "But we will need you to come to Oxford in person for an interview."

I agonized. Dorothy and I barely had enough money to put food on our table. Unfortunately, I had to turn down Oxford's generous offer.

A decade and a half after these events, I happened to be at Oxford on a research trip. It was  my first time there, and I remembered how years before I had longed to go to Oxford. Well, let me tell you, Oxford was as glorious as I had dreamed her to be! Her moody English sky hovered over stone edifices like Madame de Rênal's shawl over her summer dress.

Eventually, Dorothy and I, two penniless missionary kids at Bemidji State University, had to settle for the cheap North American version of Oxford. The University of Toronto, in Canada.

Finally, I was headed off to graduate school to become a bona fide secular academic! Finally, I would enter the inner sanctum of the intelligentsia! I would move from the hall to the bedroom of Lady Academe, like Julien in Stendhal's *Le rouge et le noir*!

SCENE 16   INTERIOR   UPSTAIRS, MAYOR'S MANSION

EXTREME CLOSEUP - JULIEN'S FACE

Julien lies in bed, eyes open. The clock strikes one. The CAMERA PULLS OUT as he gets up and leaves his bedroom. He tiptoes down the hallway and stops in front of a closed door. The CAMERA PULLS IN as Julien scratches on the door. The door opens. He walks in and the door shuts behind him.

CUT TO: WIDE SHOT – JULIEN AND MADAME DE RÊNAL

The two embrace on her bed. She is crying.

                    MADAME DE RÊNAL

        Julien! I'm ten years older than you! How
        can you love me?

"Prre-sumptuous!"

This time it was not the manager of the carpet store interrupting Stendhal's *Le rouge et le noir* looping around in my head like an endless movie. It was a British professor speaking at the University of Toronto. A British professor with a degree from Oxford University.

"It is prre-sumptuous," the professor said, rolling his "r" in that highfalutin English way, "for anyone to claim they know medieval music."

"Medieval music is ex-trre-mely difficult!"

My love affair with the world of research and scholarship began and ended with an Englishman from Buckinghamshire who had earned his doctorate at Oxford University.

Let us call him Professor Sehguh.

Professor Sehguh may not have been as inspiring or as caring as Dean Fredrikson, but his credentials sure were daunting.

Like Madame de Rênal did to young Julien, Professor Sehguh lured me into the mysteries of medieval studies. Like many of my Toronto professors, he was impressed by my having been "raised in Provence," as he put it.

Other professors were impressed by my being born in Morocco. So, I learned to play the Moroccan lute, the 'ud. Here I am, playing the 'ud as a graduate student with  my Moroccan friend Hassan. Hassan is playing the darbuka, the traditional clay drum of Morocco.

With every year of graduate studies, I sank deeper and deeper in love with Lady Academe. University was helping me re-connect with my past, with Morocco and France.

My every waking hour became consumed by Lady Academe, like Julien by Madame de Rênal.

From time to time, however, I would feel a brief chill, a foreshadowing of the end of our love affair, like Julien when he left Madame de Rênal.

SCENE 23   INTERIOR   MADAME DE RÊNAL'S BEDROOM

Julien and Madame de Rênal lie in bed. She faces just off camera, her head on the pillow. He looks animated; she is stone cold. It is their last night together.

                    JULIEN

    You've already forgotten me!

CUT TO: CLOSEUP - MADAME DE RÊNAL

A large tear runs down her right cheek.

MADAME DE RÊNAL (barely opening her mouth)

    I feel my heart freezing …

CUT TO: WIDE SHOT - THE BEDROOM WINDOW

Without kissing her, Julien gets up, dresses, goes
to the window and opens it. The heavy curtains
flare out and now we hear, faintly, the sounds of
the wind and the outdoors. He ties a knotted rope
to the window and prepares to go down.

"John!"

It was the end of my Masters' year and Guy was greeting me at the train station. Guy, my old friend from Grenoble. After eleven years away, Dorothy and I had returned to Europe.

"De retour chez toi," Guy said.

"Eh oui," I answered, "de retour chez moi."

Yes, back home in France. France, my *chez moi*. Or was it?

After a decade of not seeing each other, Guy and I talked for hours. At one point, he summed things up with a turn of phrase worthy of a newspaperman.

"You missionary kids, you are *déracinés*, uprooted."

Only later did I realize how accurately that described me as a missionary kid. *Déraciné*. Uprooted. Back in Europe after eleven years, I felt as uprooted there as I did in America.

That same spring, Dorothy and I met up with my parents, still going strong as missionaries to North Africans in France. One day, they drove us to a small village that we used to visit when I was young. After

 dinner, we walked around the hills. In front of us, my parents held hands. Suddenly, they seemed old, and suddenly I knew that all too soon I would be as old as them, and that my one regret would be that, unlike them, Dorothy and I would not – for we could not – have children of our own to walk behind us.

All for the best. I can only imagine the awkward title of my unborn child's autobiography: *Kid of a Missionary Kid: A Memoir*. Yes, probably all for the best.

On the flight back to Toronto, I decided that my time of being uprooted, *déraciné*, was over. It was time to stop fantasizing about Europe, time to embrace my North American future. Yes, it was time, because, like Julien in Stendhal's *Le rouge et le noir*, I would soon be leaving the comfort of Lady Academe. I would have to face academia's greatest challenge, that of finding a job.

Like Julien in the director's room at the Seminary in Besançon, I was about to be tested.

SCENE 25 INTERIOR THE SEMINARY AT BESANÇON

WIDE SHOT – THE SEMINARY DIRECTOR'S ROOM

Near an open window sits the seminary director Father Pirard at his desk, reading a letter. Julien stands away from the desk.

```
CUT TO: CLOSEUP - FATHER PIRARD

     I have here three hundred and twenty-one men
     who aspire to the holiest of callings.  Only
     eight have been recommended.  You will be the
     ninth.

     Loquerisme linguam latinam? (Subtitle: Can
     you speak to me in Latin?)

CUT TO: CLOSEUP - JULIEN

                    JULIEN

     Ita, pater optime.  (Subtitle: Of course,
     Reverend Father.)
```

"John Dickinson Haines."

It was graduation day and the university provost was interrupting my reverie, calling me forward to receive my diploma. Hundreds of us sat in Toronto's Convocation Hall, ready to receive our doctorates.

I walked up, took my diploma, shook the provost's hand, and sat back down. I was sandwiched between Dorothy, who was also getting her doctorate, and my classmate Bruce, who was also getting his doctorate.

"There's a lot of us in this room getting our doctorates," I told Bruce.

"How many of us do you think will get a job in academia?"

"That's a good question," Bruce answered. He looked grim.

I had finally completed a total of twelve and a half years of postsecondary education. Two years at Christian College, two years at Bible College, two and a half years at Bemidji State University, and six years at the University of Toronto.

And yet, after all that, it looked like I might not even get a job.

Following the graduation ceremony, all of us newly minted doctors were herded outside Convocation Hall for pictures. I hugged Dorothy, hanging on for dear life. Over the last year, it had begun dawning on us just how difficult it would be to find academic employment, not to mention two jobs in the same place. We scoured *The Chronicle of Higher Education* for job openings. We taped a map of North America to  the wall with pins marking the location of each job posting. We sent out letters of application in which we sang our praises, including the medieval Latin we had learned while in Toronto.

We waited. And then we graduated.

And then, in the nick of time, Hamdu lillah, I found a job! After twelve and a half years of postsecondary education, at last I had a job! A real job in academia as a professor! Finally, I would settle down, grow some roots, and leave my old missionary kid ways behind me! I would never have to think about missionaries again. Never again would I have to say goodbye.

There was one little problem. My new job was teaching at a Christian college.

SCENE 28   EXTERIOR   THE SQUARE AT BESANÇON

In a TRACKING SHOT, we follow Julien across the square where everyone is getting ready for the Feast of Corpus Christi. It's a bright day. We hear the hubbub of activity all across the square. Festive music rings out.

Julien arrives at the entrance of the cathedral and finds Father Chas-Bernard, a rotund man. Father Chas-Bernard stretches out his arms towards Julien.

CUT TO: MEDIUM SHOT - FATHER CHAS-BERNARD & JULIEN

                FATHER CHAS-BERNARD

Welcome, my son! I've been waiting for you. We've got a long day's work ahead, so let's go have some breakfast!

"John," said a voice with a southern drawl.

"It's good to finally meet you, John. Welcome to Rome, Georgia!"

TRANSPLANTED

CHAPTER 11
CHEROKEE BAPTISTS

Lady Academe had not been an ideal lover. She had seduced me away from becoming a missionary and made me waste many a night reading all manner of useless things. But one useful thing Lady Academe did accomplish. She got me my first full-time, tenure-track job.

The work in academia that I managed to get at the eleventh hour, after thirty applications sent out from California to Maine, landed me right back in the briar patch of Christian fundamentalism.

I began to work for the Southern Baptist Convention in Rome, Georgia.

I nearly didn't get a post as a professor. After a spate of rejection letters, I was granted a phone interview for a job at an evangelical school whose statement of faith included a clause on pre-millenialism which all employees had to sign. Not only was I willing to sign anything, I told them, I was a missionary kid!

I never heard from Trinity International University again.

Finally, one school offered me full-time work. It was called Shorter College.

It hadn't always been called Shorter College. Originally, the school was known as Cherokee Baptist Female College. The Cherokee people had been in and around northwest Georgia for nigh on a thousand years when one fine day the Baptists arrived. Shortly after the Baptists came the gold rush, and that's when the Cherokee people were politely asked to leave. And that's how Cherokee Baptist Female College got its name.

After the gold rush came Alfred Shorter.

Alfred Shorter was a little orphan boy who had run away from foster care in Alabama. Little Alfred crossed over into Georgia and went to work for a Mr. Baldwin up Monticello way. No one ever figured out how it happened but, next thing you know, Mr. Baldwin died and Alfred Shorter inherited $40,000 plus Mr. Baldwin's widow.

Mr. Baldwin's widow and little Alfred Shorter got married and moved plum across state to Rome, Georgia, where Mr. Shorter, as he was now called, became the town's leading businessman. Being a businessman, Mr. Shorter liked to philanthropize, and so he decided he would refurbish Cherokee Baptist Female College.

That's how it got to be called Shorter College.

I do wish that Mr. Shorter had not done that, because it made my new working place sound like a school for little people, or a place that didn't quite make the grade.

All the same, I was grateful for work at Shorter College. I tried to integrate best I could. I explained to everyone that I too was a Southerner. They had me pegged as a Yankee from the funny way I talked, but I told them my Daddy was a Southerner and I was raised in the South. The South of France, mind you, but the story of Southern France pretty much runs the same way as that of the American South. Both suffered their War of Northern Aggression.

And if all of that wasn't good enough, why, I was as good as Baptist.

My Daddy used to tell the joke about the Liberty Baptist College student who got kicked out for a hole in his bathing suit, in the *knee*, but my Daddy didn't  mean it! Truth be told, I myself had been baptized when I was sixteen years old. Full immersion. None of that papist child-sprinkling malarkey. Here I am ready to be dunked. It's a poor picture, I know, but it's all that remains from so long ago. Yes, I may have sounded Yankee, but deep down in my water-soaked heart I was a Southern Baptist crying to get out.

Shorter College sure lived up to its name. It was small, small enough to give both Dorothy and I teaching jobs, something that Lord knows only happens once in a rare and special while, as folks often reminded us then and continued to remind us long afterwards.

Dorothy loved teaching and she was mighty good at it, if I may say so. It wasn't me the college's publicity people went looking for when they needed a picture of a professor teaching. It was Dorothy.

Come to think of it, maybe the publicity folks passed me over because of the unusual clothes I put on from time to time, like this djellaba. The djellaba was for educational purposes since I needed to broaden my students' horizons with World Music. World Music being music from anywhere in the world besides northwest Georgia. In no time, I had students singing in Arabic and beating on darbukas.

Now, where was I? Oh yes, the Shorter publicity people taking pictures of Dorothy teaching. Well, see for yourself. There she is, teaching in the great out of doors, right on the lawn of the campus' main entrance for all to see. Ain't she something? I can tell you that the students loved her to pieces. Why, they learned a lot from their Dr. Dorothy, a moniker that may sound cheeky to you Yankees but one that is in fact the ultimate Southern expression of endearment and respect.

When I was a young boy growing up in the Old South – the South of France, like I said before – my Daddy would sit me on his knee and tell me stories about his childhood in Petersburg, Virginia. My Daddy told some very fine stories and sang some very fine songs, which I enjoyed very much. One song he had learned from his own Daddy. (That would be my Grandpappy.) The song went like this:

> If every star was a little pickaninny
> And there was a little chicken in the moon,
> There would be no light
> And every night
> Each star would take a knife and fork and spoon ...

I had no idea what a pickaninny was, but I just loved that song. That pickaninny song ran in my head for hours.

Some of the stories my Daddy told Joy and me came from a book called the Great Book of Uncle Remus.

I had no idea who Uncle Remus was, but, boy oh boy, could that man tell a yarn, notwithstanding his speech impediment. The way my Daddy imitated him, Uncle Remus talked with a special Southern American accent that left off all the endings of words and also sounded unusually happy and gregarious. It was weird, but I loved how Uncle Remus talked.

All the stories from Uncle Remus seemed to revolve around one animal – and I loved animals! – whose name was Brer Rabbit.

To this day I still haven't figured out whether Brer Rabbit wanted to go in the briar patch or whether he wanted to stay out of it, but that old Brer Rabbit, he just fired up my imagination.

None of you readers, not even you Innocent Ones, can imagine my delight when I discovered that by moving to Georgia, I had moved to the home of Brer Rabbit. Dorothy rolled her eyes, as she sometimes does, when I insisted that we pay a visit to Brer Rabbit down in Nowhere, Georgia.

When I got there, I found out that Uncle Remus was not the author of Uncle Remus' Great Book after all. He was a slave who had told his stories to a boy named Mr. Joel Chandler Harris. Mr. Joel Chandler Harris then moved to Atlanta and made lots of money

 publishing these stories. Dorothy rolled her eyes one more time as I explained all of this, but I didn't care! I still loved Uncle Remus and Brer Rabbit. To prove it, I had my picture taken next to the statue of Brer Rabbit at the Joel Chandler Harris Museum in Nowhere, Georgia. Dorothy took this picture, if you must know, somewhat against her volition.

You clever Believers have probably guessed that Mr. Joel Chandler Harris was white and Uncle Remus was black. You've probably also guessed that black

people were in short supply at Shorter College. I was never exactly sure of the reason for this, since we Southerners generally tend towards politeness and good manners, much more so than uncouth Yankees.

With the odd exception, of course.

One day, a black female student came up to Dorothy after class and burst out crying. This student had been sitting quietly in her dorm room when the phone rang. When she answered it, this is what she heard:

"I'm gonna kill you, nigger."

What was that, Believer? Outrageous, you say? Oh, you Unbelievers and Innocent Readers agree?

Well, before you Yankees get yourselves all worked up, let's not forget who started up the slave trade in the first place. It wasn't us Southerners, no sir! Let's not forget that it was a King from Europe, from Portugal to be precise, who first sent his ships to Africa to collect slaves. Let's not forget, too, that the slave trade's main port of calls at the time – Martinique, Jamaica, and so forth – were owned and operated by Europeans, not Americans. Let's not forget either that, in the early 1700s, the State of Georgia had actually forbidden the import of slaves, and that the main trading station was Newport, Rhode Island. Rhode Island, if I'm not mistaken, is Yankee territory. Yes, sir, *everyone*'s got blood on their hands when it comes to the African slave trade.

At Shorter College, we did have ourselves some mighty fine black students, one of whom I remember very well.

Her name was Zipporah Gibbs.

I believe that Zipporah is the name of the wife of Moses, so you know Zipporah Gibbs came from a good Christian family.

Now Zipporah Gibbs wasn't just black. She was *black*, if you know what I mean. She wasn't Barack-Obama-half-tone black. There was no plantation owner's son somewhere in her family tree. No sir, Zipporah Gibbs was one-hundred-percent black and the Shorter publicity folks loved Zipporah Gibbs. On every college brochure and poster and what have you, for the duration of Zipporah's four-year baccalaureate at Shorter College and then  some, there was a picture of beautiful young Zipporah Gibbs, singing her little heart out. Us white folks loved Zipporah Gibbs to pieces. And I do believe the feeling was mutual.

Maybe I exaggerated just now the wonders of the South, of Zipporah Gibbs and of Brer Rabbit. Maybe I inflated the open-mindedness of Southern Baptists and the braveness of the Cherokee. It may be too that, looking back this many years later, my time at Shorter College seems rosier than it actually was.

Truth is, I was as restless at Shorter College as a djellaba-wearing missionary kid climbing up a palm tree!

The Christian climate at Shorter may have been watered down by my parents' standards, but it was downright suffocating at times. As suffocating as a Georgia summer afternoon. There was weekly chapel, prayer at faculty meetings, Bible this and Bible that. Same old same-oh. Why, even the school logo had a big fat Bible smack dab in the middle!

As usual, the instinct to say goodbye kicked in.

One of the ways in which I prepared for my escape from Shorter's Baptist prison and out into the big leagues of academia, was to educate myself on the subject of cocktails.

You Innocent Readers probably can't understand this, but when it came to cocktails, we missionary kids were taught mainly one thing: if you drank cocktails, you were going straight to hell.

On his honeymoon, my young missionary father refused to even eat in one restaurant because they served alcohol. The only alcohol my missionary parents ever drank in France was at communion, and that was just to pacify confused French Believers who could not have imagined their communion with good old Baptist grape juice.

The first full glass of wine I had was during my Bible School days in Bemidji, and it tasted pretty good. It wasn't until I started working for the Southern Baptist Convention that I graduated from wine to higher spirits, by which I mean more highly distilled spirits.

Don't be upset, Believers. I needed to do this for professional reasons. I needed to be able to sit down with the heathen at an academic conference dinner and nonchalantly ask for a Bombay Gin martini with Triple Sec, ice and a little lemon peel on the side, thank you very much, and make it look as if it was the most natural thing in the world.

It isn't the most natural thing in the world, because I now know that that is *not* how you make a classic martini. Gin with a splash of Martini Sec and Martini Rosso. That's how you make a martini. I know this because I worked very hard at the School of Cocktails, and I began my education with the martini.

The Liquor Store in Rome, Georgia was a windowless box run by someone who may well have been an illegal immigrant.

"Hello, my friend," the manager would say as I walked into the Liquor Store.

"Hello, again," I would answer, looking down at the floor nervously.

I would shuffle over to the closest shelf, deliberate for as short a time as possible and scoop up a few bottles of wine.

"That's it for today?" would ask the Liquor Store manager.

"Yes, that's it," I would answer, glancing at the door and hoping that no one from Shorter College would come in.

One day, I decided to buy my first bottle of gin at the Liquor Store.

"What do you recommend for gin?" I asked the Liquor Store manager in a way that let him know I had to leave the Liquor Store very soon.

"Bombay Gin, of course," the Liquor Store manager replied.

His endorsement of Bombay Gin seemed suspect to me because he looked like he came from Bombay, but I figured it was worth a try. Pretty soon I was mixing a martini with the best of them. Over the years I perfected my cocktail skills, as you can see in this picture of my very own version of a Mary Pickford. And if you don't know what a Mary Pickford is, why, you come on over sometime  and I'll make you one. Everyone likes a Mary Pickford, including our missionary kid visitors.

There can be no doubt that I took the South for granted, and I have missed it in one way or the other every single day since I left it. The South very nearly became my home.

It would have been nice, now that I think of it, to settle down in Rome, Georgia and finally grow some roots.

I was so anxious to leave Shorter College back then, and now that I've left it, I can't rightly remember why. I believe it had something to do with foolish ambition. Just for that, I left many a precious thing behind.

Too late now. I guess that's just part of growing old and having more regrets than you know what to do with.

"I'm very sorry to see you leave," one of my Shorter colleagues told me.

"Even though it was sort of inevitable," she added.

I cringed, but she just kept right on going.

"I think there's some poem about a person leaving 'us' who wasn't really 'ours', but I forget what it was," she continued. "Probably one of those maudlin things about a dead child."

Folks, that is exactly what she said, and I can tell you looking back on it that I had no idea what to make of it but somehow it feels as significant to me now as the Cherokee Trail of Tears or the Seven Hills of Rome, Georgia.

Like little Alfred Shorter leaving Eufaula, Alabama, I was taking my leave of Rome, Georgia.

Finally, finally, finally, I was saying goodbye to the Christian scene. No more Baptists, no more missionaries. And no more missionary kid.

No, sir. I was heading off for the big leagues of secular academia.

CHAPTER 12

THE INDUSTRY OF ACADEMIA

If you are reading these words, then more than likely you have paid into the industry of academia. Maybe you know a student. Maybe you work at a college. Maybe you work in one of the many industries that feeds the industry of academia, like the sporting equipment industry. Either way, you have paid your dues to one of the largest industries in the world.

Little did I know what a perfect preparation my missionary kid past had been for a career in the industry of academia!

For one, there was the bookishness. When it came to the Bible, we missionary kids were bookish in the extreme. One game we used to play was called "sword drill," the sword being the Bible. We would sit down with our swords in our laps, ready to fling them open.

"Haggai 2:8!" someone would cry out.

As fast as we could, we'd open our Bibles to find the book of Haggai. For some reason, the winner of these sword drills was always a girl.

"'The silver is mine and the gold is mine', declares the Lord of Hosts," she would read out, and we'd move on to the next sword drill.

Beyond the Bible, our readings were often equally eloquent. Sometimes they were downright incomprehensible. Take the following passage from A.W. Tozer's *Of God and Men* (1960):

> The Bible is among other things a book of revealed truth ... Certain facts are revealed that could not be discovered by the most brilliant mind. These facts are of such a nature as to be past finding out.

I don't know about you Innocent Ones, but the more I read these three sentences just now, the less I understand them. This high-minded prose was the kind of thing we missionary kids read on a regular basis. We also spoke King James.

"I felt the Lord's leading," we would say.

Or, "I am following my Word for today."

Yes, as a missionary kid I was made for academia!

I had been trained in all the right things: the power of institutions, the riddles of the word and the fellowship of the few.

And here I thought that by joining the big leagues of academia I had finally rid myself of all things Christian! I was about to find out that the secular industry of academia was much more religious than I could ever have imagined.

162

Academia, dear Innocent Ones, dear Believers and Unbelievers, is a church. I did not say it is *like* a church. No, academia *is* a church. It's a religion. To join it, you have to believe.

Academia is a church. It has its infallible texts. It has its unquestioned authorities. It also has its mystical language, its separation from the world, its dispensations of wisdom to the un-doctored masses, its secret rites of initiation, its code of shaming, and, above all, its endless demands on the converted few devoted to a holy calling of perpetual service.

The global industry of academia is kind of like a giant pyramid.

At the bottom of the pyramid are the staff that run academia. Then come the undergraduates, the "basic income units" (yes, that is what they are called at my university), most of whom never finish, which saves the industry a lot of money. Near the middle of the pyramid are the graduate students.

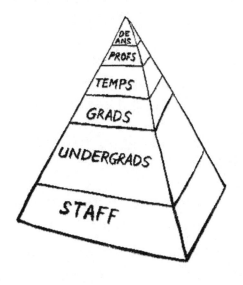

A minority of these go on to become low-paid adjunct professors for as long as they can stand it. And at the very top are the fortunate few, the deans and the tenured professors, and that includes yours truly, whether I like to admit it or not.

If you don't believe me about academia being a church, take a look at the most prestigious university  near you. Does it or does it not look like a medieval cathedral? As an example, here is a picture I took of the building where I once gave a talk at Indiana University.

By the way, giving a talk at a prestigious university is not as impressive a feat as it sounds. Basically, here is how it came to pass, to borrow a phrase from the King James Bible.

"So, John," said my Indiana University colleague over beers at a conference one day, "how about giving a talk at Indiana University?"

"Sounds good to me," I said, burping up beer bubbles.

A few beers later and a few months after that, I was giving a talk at Indiana University. The congregants sat in their seats, I was presented with great pomp, and then I gave my talk, roughly the length of a sermon.

There's another pyramid in the church of academia, and I would draw this one for you too, except I'm tired of drawing academic pyramids.

This pyramid's the one of all the universities and colleges in the world. At the top are Harvard, Princeton and Yale. I don't need to tell you that Shorter College was the lowest in the pyramid of all the schools in Georgia, and possibly in the United States of America. Many of my Shorter colleagues got so worked up about this that they left Shorter College.

So did I, and let me tell you how it happened.

First of all, you should know that every year tens of thousands of people get a doctorate. Only a tiny portion of them ever get a job in academia. As a result, the lucky stiffs employed as tenured professors are pretty defensive and generally ill-disposed to others of their kind.

Professors like to rant about how bad their fellow professors are. One of my favorite such rants is a book called *Some of My Best Friends Are Professors*, published in 1958.

"The inter-departmental throat-cuttings," declares the author of this book, "are incredible to the outsider."

This is because every academic in training wants to be a research professor, he explains.

"Ruthless," is what the research professor must be, "so that he can devote all his time to publishing his little articles at regular intervals."

Most professors never make the research grade, and so, concludes the author of *Some of My Best Friends Are Professors*, these failed researchers become "popularizers who try to make their classes as fascinating as a basketball game."

Being a professor at Shorter College, I was definitely a popularizer!

I had to wear several hats. Not just the academic one, as you can see in this picture, but the hat of an entertainer, of an avuncular counselor, of a devoted teacher and of an all-around eccentric. If, however, I wanted to become a research professor, I would need to publish. That's what I was told, anyways.

"Publish, publish, publish," a senior professor at Harvard once advised me early on in my professorial career.

And so, I did.

Now that I have half dozen books to my name and a few more on the way, as well as three edited volumes, sixty chapters and articles in encyclopedia-type works, and well over thirty essays in peer-reviewed journals, I have to confess that I, a lowly missionary kid who somehow became a full professor in the industry of academia, have no idea how academic publishing works.

Like the eucharist, academic publishing is a mystery.

Here is how academic publishing is supposed to work. A well written article or book on a well researched topic is submitted to an academic journal. Over the next six months or so, this submission is reviewed by two or three of the greatest experts in the field. It's called peer review, and the name of the submission's author is withheld so as to ensure impartiality. These two or three experts then decide, yes or no, whether this anonymous book or essay will get published.

That's how academic publishing is supposed to work.

When I submitted my first essay for publication, the journal's editor sent back a hand-scribbled note.

"We would like to use your piece in our forthcoming issue," it went, ending with: "Is this satisfactory to you?"

No peer review, no waiting around for months. My first published essay just sailed through and was published immediately.

Maybe this had to do with its subject, a scholarly squabble that resulted in death by sword fight. Also, it was an English journal that accepted it. I decided to stick with English publishers and fencing stories, and managed a handful more essays and one book on the topic, and I have been grateful to the English ever since and to sword fighters everywhere.

Just kidding. I have published on other things besides fencing scholars.

For my first edited book, I collaborated with a colleague who proposed that we produce a volume of essays in honor of Professor Sehguh, whom I mentioned to you earlier. We drew up a list of twelve contributors, a standard number for such a volume.

We then passed this list by Professor Sehguh himself. That was a mistake!

"Only twelve contributors!" Professor Sehguh exclaimed, looking at the roster of stellar contributors.

"It does make it look as though one does not have much of a following," he said. (That's an exact quote, by the way.)

Professor Sehguh then proceeded to suggest no less than sixty people to celebrate his glorious self. By the time I had finished with that volume four years later, I swore to never edit a volume again.

I went on to edit three more, and I'm about to edit another one.

For those of you aspiring to be academic researchers, I have no other advice than to brace yourself for interruptions like the cat shown lying here in front of my computer screen, distracting me from writing one more impenetrable sentence. His name was Joey, and he was the most affectionate cat I have ever known. I should have turned off the computer right then and there, and put little Joey on my lap, because now Joey's

dead and I can't even remember anymore what important thing I was writing at the time.

And besides, I doubt that any of you have ever read it.

Which makes me wonder if I shouldn't have become a missionary rather than a professor. Too late now! Like I said at the end of the previous chapter on my time with the Cherokee Baptists, that's just what happens when you grow old and have more regrets than you know what to do with.

Like the missionary, the academic migrates from one place to the other, especially if he or she aspires to be a research professor.

Goodbye, always goodbye.

At Shorter College, I began learning the ruthless ways of the academic migrant. I got a job offer at the University of North Texas, threatened to leave, and Shorter College gave me a raise.

Then came the announcement for the job in Toronto to replace Professor Sehguh who was retiring. Many applied, including myself. One of the hopefuls was a man who was ten years my senior. Let's call this man Professor Reirg.

The year that this job was posted, Professor Reirg's wife, a sizable woman whose parents had made their fortune in the pickle business, cornered

Professor Sehguh at an academic conference. I happened to be there, standing off at a distance.

"Blah-BLAH-blah," was all I heard her say.

Visibly distressed, Professor Sehguh pretended to listen to her, backing away.

"Blah-BLAH-blah, blaah-BLAH-BLAAH!"

Professor Reirg's wife was berating Professor Sehguh for not giving her husband special consideration on account at his having taught at Yale. At one point, she caught me staring at her.

"Who is this person?" she said, not so much a question as a snarl.

She had no idea at the time that "this person" was the one who was about to take the job out from under her husband's nose.

I don't have to tell you, especially you Believers, that I was made to pay for the privilege of usurping  Professor Reirg in a currency beloved by religious and academics alike: humiliation. Thankfully, I was used to humiliation from my days in French school. Here I am on the first day of school with my sister Joy, both of us wearing a jacket that the French call a *tablier*. You can't tell from this picture, since it's black and white, but my *tablier* was dark pink. For one whole year at school, I was made to wear pink.

By the time the Toronto job came around, I was used to humiliation.

In preparation for the on-campus interview, Professor Sehguh, who incidentally was on the hiring committee to replace himself (unprecedented), told me to read as many times as possible the longest book he had written. During the two-day interview, I was given a document to study with an oral examination promised at the end (also unprecedented). With Professor Sehguh as the main examiner, I failed. After the dean offered me the job a few hours later, I waited a few weeks before signing the contract.

Professor Sehguh was livid.

"I have five words for you," he told me on the phone.

"'Don't-play-hard-to-get.'"

Technically speaking, "'Don't-play-hard-to-get" is six words, but never mind.

By the skin of my teeth, or so it seemed to me then, I got the job.

That, dear reader, is how this American missionary kid, born and bred in the briar patch of evangelical anti-intellectualism, a dropout of both Christian liberal arts school and Bible college, with no other pedigree than the articles and books he managed to publish all on his own, by sheer will and good luck, yes, that is how this un-pedigreed missionary kid came to replace an Oxford-educated Englishman at one of the world's leading research universities.

I think you'll agree, that's a pretty amazing story. But not an unlikely one.

And that, dear reader – dear Believer, Unbeliever and Innocent One – is also how I, a missionary kid raised on the shores of the Mediterranean, uprooted to the French Alps, to Germany and finally to America, that is how this wandering missionary kid ended up transplanted in Canada.

CHAPTER 13

A WOMAN FROM CANADA

There once was a woman from Canada named Hannah. Hannah lived a long time ago, so I never knew her, but believe it or not, Hannah from Canada was my great-grandmother.

Me, a pye-dog missionary kid, I always took comfort in the fact that at least I was completely American: both of my parents one-hundred-percent American. But then I found out that my American pedigree had a flaw! You see, my mother may have been born and bred in the United States, but both of her parents were born and bred in Canada. So, technically speaking, that makes me half Canadian. An American-Canadian bastard.

This so worried me that I decided to go with Mom and check out the home of her Canadian parents. There we stood, she and I, in the one-room schoolhouse in Fenwick, Nova Scotia, where my twenty-two-year-old grandmother Minnie once taught the teenage boy who ten years later would become her husband. On the wall of the old schoolhouse hung a photograph of a group of students. There, in the front row, demure and a little hunched over but nestled close to a cheery boy, was my mother's Dad, as if not one of those one hundred years since had elapsed.

"What a magical moment," my mother whispered.

When I think of my mother's grandmother, the woman I was just telling you about, Hannah from Canada, it's the Scottish poet Robert Burns that comes to mind, for Hannah had Scottish blood. Yes, I think of Burns and of his famous poem, "Auld Lang Syne," and when I think of "Auld Lang Syne," I think of the souls of the dearly departed. They sing to me a whyles, especially on nights when I've had a glass of whisky. Canadian whisky, such as I am drinking right now.

> Should auld acquaintance be forgot
> And never brought to mind?
> Should auld acquaintance be forgot,
> And auld lang syne!

The way it went, dear reader, was that Hannah's mother Rebeccah begat Hannah (to speak King James), Hannah begat Minnie, and Minnie begat two girls, my Mom and her sister.

People say that a family's name belongs to the man, since he's the important one, but it's the woman that gives birth to the man, not the reverse! Woman's the one who raises the man and cleans up after his wars! Woman it is who decides when enough is enough, when the time is right to lay down by the river and sleep. When I picture Hannah sleeping the long sleep, well, it brings to my mind another song by Robbie Burns, the one he wrote to the River Afton.

My Mary's asleep by the murmuring stream,
Flow gently sweet Afton, disturb not her dream.

Hannah was by all accounts a remarkable woman, but it's Hannah's husband got the credit. "Whenever he spoke," said the preacher at Hannah's husband's funeral, "people felt that he had an authentic message from God."

Oh, he was a spiritual man, Hannah's husband! Two years later, when it was Hannah's turn to die, struck down by a stroke from a lifetime of doing her husband's work, no one spoke of her with such high-minded reverence! No one did, but they should have, because, believe me, she had hard-working Scottish blood running in her veins. Her parents had come from Scotland to settle on the shores of a land so overrun by Scots that they called it Nova Scotia.

As a girl, Hannah loved to listen to her Da tell the lore and poetry of his native Scotland, especially the poems of Scotland's favorite son Robert Burns. Hannah so fell in love with poetry that she became a schoolteacher, and might have remained a schoolteacher for the rest of her life, but for one thing. Aye, one thing! You see, Hannah was cursed with a woman's burden, a burden  that lies heavier with some than with others. Many call it a blessing, but I say it's a curse. How else can I say it? Hannah was beautiful.

175

To be beautiful means to be looked at by men. And this, for better or for worse, but often for worse, means marriage. So, along came the man I mentioned earlier, the lucky stiff that got Hannah. This man was no catch, believe me! Hannah's man loved to talk as men do, like me blathering on right now with a glass of whisky in my hand, but he was as sickly as a mangy beaver. The sickness went to his legs and head, and it made him dizzy and bedridden for much of his life.

He did, however, find the energy to get Hannah pregnant seven times. Each time the seed took, and each time the child survived and had to be cared for by Hannah while her man rested from his sickness. Aye, all seven children lived to a ripe old age.

Hannah had her revenge, however, for each and every one of the seven children was a girl. There wasn't a man child in the lot.

Rebecca begat Hannah, and Hannah begat Minnie. Seven girls, all married but two by the time they reached their late twenties. That was Minnie and Mary, the inseparable two. The old man sick as a mangy beaver and mother out working the farm! So, it was left to Mary and Minnie to care for the old man. Finally, he decided to die, and two years later Hannah did too. Minnie, like her mother Hannah,

loved the poetry of Robbie Burns, and like her mother she had taken to teaching. Minnie had seen firsthand just how much trouble a husband could be and she decided the troubles of a husband were not worth it.

This was the mid-1920s, dear reader, with no thought to the coming calamity! Then came the Stock Market Crash followed by the Great Depression.

"Crash!" like the nest in Burns' "Poem to a Mouse," the one he wrote after turning up a mouse nest with a plough. That's why they call him the Ploughman Poet, don't you know!

The Best laid schemes o' mice an' men gang aft agley,
An' lea'e us nought but grief an' pain, for promis'd joy!

After the Stock Market Crash, free-thinking women resorted to taking husbands. The man who presented himself to Minnie at that very late moment, for she was fully thirty-two years of age, this man had once been her student in a one-room schoolhouse in Fenwick, Nova Scotia. This simple, hardworking man, had been waiting in the wings ever since he first laid eyes on his teacher and was "touched by love," as he recalled many years later.

A man of few words, unused to affection, but available at the right moment.

They were married. Times were hard. Minnie's man took Minnie away from Canada. West to Washington State, east to Maryland, and finally south to Florida.

But all this time, Minnie never lost sight of her beloved Canada. And Minnie made sure that all three of her children didn't either, and that they knew the stories of Nova Scotia and the songs of the legendary Robbie Burns.

Minnie had one son and two daughters. It's the daughters I wish to tell you of, not the son. One of Minnie's daughters in particular.

Her name, if you must know, was Frances.

Hannah begat Minnie, and Minnie begat Frances. Out of Minnie's womb Fran came into this world, but this world was too little for her. When she left her mortal body behind, Fran returned to where she'd come, to the light of the eyes of God.

"How joyously happy my life has been" she told me once, "constantly spent in the presence of Jesus."

Even as a child, Fran had something of the other-worldly. She had a tall, thin body and a tower of a neck that cradled her aquiline face. What a face my Aunt Fran had, with that smile,  that holy smile! Looking at her in the front of this picture, with her two siblings, Fran seems about to burst into a peal of holy laughter!

Fran answered the missionary call. She even persuaded her little sister Peggy to do the same. For a time, Fran worked with various missions, and that's how she got to Canada. Eventually Fran broke away from mission organizations to live entirely by faith in the Eastern Townships of Quebec as an independent missionary.

As her poverty grew, Fran's body weakened.

Why Fran had picked Quebec when she knew so little French did make her sister Peggy wonder! Why Quebec? Fran could have gone to a normal mission field like Morocco, where Peggy worked, Peggy whom Fran visited shortly before  settling in Canada. Here you can see Minnie's two missionary daughters standing in a Moroccan souk in the summer of 1965.

In a poem found in her things after her passing, Fran made clear the reason for her peculiar mission field choice, Canada:

Canada, the place of my parents' birth,
Where trees and woods spread over the earth.
Now it's my gentle and peaceable home,
Where from deep in my heart there flows a poem.

My Aunt Fran came to visit my missionary family in Casablanca in July 1965. It was her first plane flight. I  had just turned one. This picture shows Fran holding me in front of our apartment in Casablanca's Quartier Polo, on the Rue de l'Hérault, number five, which number you can see if you look closely near the top of the gate. From the start, Fran and I shared a special bond. It was as if Fran could see into my soul, as if she understood the spiritual turmoil that has plagued me my whole life long. She understood this turmoil for having experienced it herself.

In 1975, when I was eleven, she wrote a poem entitled "To Johnny." Here is an excerpt:

> The how, the when, the where, the why
> Could sometimes almost make you cry.
> Answers are there, you are very sure,
> But truth and light seem never pure.

When at last you passed from this world, dear Fran, you had no earthly husband or lover to mourn you, only your blessed Jesus whose face you finally saw!

And so, I'll grieve you now, me, a lowly missionary kid, your nephew and your friend whose soul you understood.

For my eulogy, I'll borrow the words from that great poet Robbie Burns:

Fare thee weel, my only Luve!
And fare thee weel, a while!
And I will come again, my Luve,
Tho' it were ten thousand mile!

It was almost exactly a year after Fran's Casablanca visit, in August 1966, that I first met my maternal grandmother Minnie. Mom's admiration for her mother Minnie had preceded the arrival of this strong, strong woman who had made my own mother so strong. During those three weeks of her visit to our little Casablanca apartment, my grandmother took up with me a habit she had passed on to her two daughters.

Reading!

Aye, Gram Minnie loved to read! And me, I loved to listen to her stories! I listened very, very carefully.

Maybe it's the whisky gone to my head just now, or maybe the many years that have passed since that

time, but I can't rightly remember what Minnie was reading to me in the photograph you have before you. Maybe it was from one of her favorite authors, Lucy Maud Montgomery, whose home in Leaskdale, Ontario, incidentally, lies only a mile from the desk where I am typing these words.

Regardless, Minnie's love of reading, along with my family's fanaticism for the Bible, helped feed the unhealthy fire of my love for the printed book and its seductive words.

Eventually I fell in love with history, and eventually I became a historian.

Eventually, too, I became a Canadian. I now live, as I just told you, down the road from the little village where Lucy Maud Montgomery wrote most of her legendary stories about Anne of Green Gables.

As she had for my Aunt Fran, and as she had for Hannah's Scottish parents, Canada took in this migrant missionary kid.

It took me a while, but in due course I became a Canadian citizen.

This, as you've guessed by now, was the sixth happy Twist of Fate in my life.

Becoming Canadian.

Gram Minnie played a part in this too. Over a year before her Casablanca visit, on the first Christmas of my life, I received from my grandmother a gift that I still treasure to this day. It was a jacket that she had sewed for me. It had matching shorts and socks, all with the same pattern: dark blue squares framed by green bars and bright yellow lines. This pattern was the tartan of Nova Scotia,

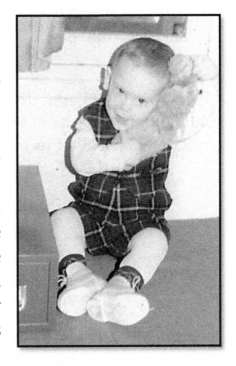

officially adopted as that province's emblem in 1963. I received the jacket the following year.

Inside this Nova Scotian jacket of mine is a lining made of satin cloth. And sewed onto this satin lining is a small tag on which are written the following words.

"Hand fashioned by Minnie Dickinson."

You see, dear reader, the past is never far from any of us. Its presence has a way of growing as more and more time goes by.

Like a continuous but imperceptible whisper, the past is always there. Like the everlasting music of the cosmos that one ceases to hear after hearing it for so long, the past weaves in and out of consciousness.

It may fade, but it never disappears.

Wherever we are, wherever we go, no matter how long we ignore it and no matter how hard we try to shake it, the past has been waiting, patiently waiting.

Lying quiet and breathing still, it has been waiting for that moment when, finally, we give in and embrace it with all of its fury and affection.

Should auld acquaintance be forgot
And never brought to mind?
Should auld acquaintance be forgot,
And auld lang syne!

CHAPTER 14
HOME

Hear now, oh reader, Believer and Unbeliever alike, and you, Innocent One, innocent of goodbyes and other religious crimes too sad and long to relate no matter how long the book, hear now of my final Twist of Fate! The seventh twist, the perfect twist. For seven is the number of perfection.

Al Hamdu lillah – Praise be to God!

Let us thank God, the Beneficent and Merciful One, whose existence lies beyond the long and sad history of humankind!

Hamdu lillah! Praise be to God!

In the month of October, in the Year of Our Lord 2010, Dorothy and I made our exodus from the metropolis of Toronto and, on the fringes of the city, by a wood, on a hilly land that once belonged to the Huron-Wendat people and that reminded us of the hills of the Black Forest where we had first met, we found our home.

It is here in my newfound Canadian home that I have learned the wonders of the shovel.

When a man has tired of the pen, he will turn to the shovel. He will start with a prayer, the first timid tear into the earth's surface, and he will fall into the rhythm of the dig until a hole is dug and well dug. From the first hole to the last one, the shovel will accompany the man all of his life.

Yes, when a man has tired of the pen, he will turn to the shovel, and he will marvel at what the shovel can teach.

What does the shovel teach, you ask, incredulous Believer? Let me tell you!

The shovel teaches life, when the hole receives the baby seed transplanted from the safety of its pot to the big outdoors. The shovel teaches endurance, when the trench is long and the man's shoulders ache at night. The shovel teaches death, when the grave is made through tears, the grave that receives the warm body of the animal who lived alongside the man as a good friend.

Others can have their Paris with its suffocating streets, their London with its acid skies, their Toronto with its temples of steel!

Me, I'll take my chances with my shovel under an open sky!

Home, then, is where the shovel is. But home is also where live the ghosts of the past.

In recent years, I have had the privilege of returning to my different homes and visiting these ghosts. After each visit, the time invariably comes to leave, and I feel my lower lip tremble at the thought of goodbye. But then I remember that each one of these places is sewn onto my heart like my grandmother's tag onto the satin lining of my Nova Scotia jacket. Even if I never see any of them again, their memory is always with me, sewn onto the lining of my heart.

How quickly time has passed between my recent visits to each one of these places and the time when once I lived in them as their indigenous son!

And yet, how slowly, how very slowly time used to pass when I was a child living in Morocco and France! How long I waited through those endless hours when Joy and I accompanied our parents on their visits to homes, homes that smelled of henna and saffron, homes like that of Kinza in Rabat, with her children milling around, and Joy and I  expected to play with them! Those visits went on, year after year, in Casablanca, Rabat, Salé, Marseille, Grenoble.

How quickly time has gone now that I stop to look back! Now the fear sets in, the knowledge of how little time is left. I reach out to swipe at the tail of time, to coax it onto my lap just a little longer. But like an extinct creature, time eludes me and is gone.

Let me tell you of my recent trip to the Black Forest.

"Lieber Herr Doktor Professor Haines," a Swiss university wrote me one day, "would you like to speak at a conference in Basel for which we will pay for both your travel and your stay?"

Why not, I said.

After giving my paper, as we say in academia, I met up with my good *ami* Guy, his wife Muriel and their two children, Mathis and Iris.

"We should go to your old school in the Black Forest," Guy said the following day. "It's only twenty minutes away."

We soon found ourselves winding through the Black Forest around lunchtime. We stopped at the village of Holzen where I had biked on many an afternoon to visit Dottie at the girl's dorm.

"You know," Guy told me, "I have never had German food."

"Well, let's go to the local Gasthaus," I said. "We'll have some Schnitzel and Spätzle! You're bound to love it!"

We walked in to the Gasthaus and sat down.

Using my imperfect German, I ordered the pride of German cooking, a duo of deep fried Wiener Schnitzel and Spätzle noodles served with a pint of homebrewed beer. The Gasthaus at Holzen, however, specialized in watery bottled beer, undercooked Schnitzel, and big yellow greasy French fries. Not a Spätzle noodle in sight.

"Impressionnant – Impressive," Guy finally managed.

With full bellies, we climbed back into the car and continued down the hill from Holzen to the

village of Bad Riedlingen, my home during boarding school days at the Black Forest Academy. As we approached, the old building looked no different than it had thirty years before when I had stood with my father for the picture that you saw earlier in this book. We stepped up to the front door. I posed for a picture with Guy's son Mathis, holding him closely, just as Dad would have held me if he'd been there.

"Rentre, John – Go in, John," Mathis nudged me.

I opened the front door of my old dorm. Nothing had changed.

Grenoble had been my home before the Black Forest, and I have been fortunate to return there more than once for academic research. About ten years ago, I sat in the archives of the Grenoble library and transcribed an Old French parchment version of Christ's Passion.

"A oreisuns s'encline el munt li pius Jesus," went the medieval text: "On the mountain, the pious Jesus bows down in prayer."

As I sat transcribing these words, I regularly looked up to gaze at the mountains all around, the same mountains my father had praised in a Prayer Letter after first coming to Grenoble.

"It does something for our spirit," he had written, "to lift up our eyes unto the hills!"

On another occasion, I went up to the mountains of Grenoble to consult some medieval books at the Grande Chartreuse Monastery, home of the world-famous herb liqueur called Chartreuse. The sign at the monastery entrance forbids visitors to enter.

"On ne visite pas le monastère," reads the sign at the monastery entrance. "No one is permitted to visit the monastery."

I went in.

My host was a very old monk who never left me out of his sight while I handled the medieval books. At one point, I explained to him that I had in my possession a camera that took pictures which could be viewed right away. I was hoping to take a picture of a medieval book.

The very old monk stared at my camera in disbelief. How, he wondered, was it possible to take pictures and view them right away?

"Could I take a picture of this medieval book while you hold it?" I asked.

"Sure," shrugged the very old monk.

I didn't dare train the camera on the dear old man, except for once, when I backed up enough so  that his two hands could be seen, each one as marvellously worn as a knotty oak tree. I didn't show him this picture after I took it, and I feel guilty about showing it to you here, but I suspect it's OK because more than likely the very old monk is free of this world by now.

After I had taken the picture, the very old monk and I talked a while. I was surprised to learn that this hermit from the Grande Chartreuse monastery in the mountains above Grenoble did not come from that part of France.

He came from the south, from the city of Marseille.

When I think back to my childhood as the son of American missionaries working in foreign lands, one place seems to me the most like home. This is Marseille.

Despite the bullying from Antoine Cilia that I told you about, some of my sweetest memories are those of *le club* where Mom and Dad spent their days trying to convert the sons and daughters of North African immigrants living in the HLMs of Marseille's thirteenth district. Here in this picture you can see my father on the far right, with boys wearing bell-bottom jeans pretending to be interested in what Dad is telling them.

Almost twenty years ago now, I returned to Marseille. I was researching a book on troubadours.

The music scene in Marseille had changed quite a bit since the days of my childhood favorite, Alain Souchon and his hit "Allô, Maman bobo." The latest fad was French rap-reggae, and I had managed to get an interview for my book with Marseille's hottest rap-reggae band, Massilia Sound System. I was sitting with the leader of Massilia Sound System at his beachfront home, when he reached over to open a drawer.

"T'en veux?" he said as he pulled out some pot and rolled it into a cigarette. "You want some?"

"Non, merci," I said. "No thanks."

He shrugged, as the French often do, and started puffing away.

The more he smoked, the better the interview went. At one point he admitted that, although he was the leader of Marseille's most popular rap group, he was not from Marseille. He wasn't even from the South of France. He was born and raised in Paris.

What a strange world, I thought. Me, an American missionary kid raised in Marseille, I had more authentic Southern French credentials than the lead singer of Massilia Sound System!

There are the places we remember. And then there is the place whose memory is hidden from our consciousness precisely because it is the most important.

The first place, the place of origin. Morocco.

Of Morocco, only a few things remain in my conscious memory, like the earthquake you heard about earlier. Little more than this. And yet, even after leaving Morocco at the age of five, that country continued to weave in and out of my life thanks to my parents' work over the next thirty years with North African immigrants in France.

Morocco had been my first place. It was the place that taught me how the world should be felt and seen. Morocco raised and nurtured me, and ever since then Morocco has never stopped calling me home.

A few years ago, for my fiftieth birthday, I returned to my Moroccan home with my faithful Dorothy at my side.

She and I retraced the steps taken by my parents fifty years before when two young American missionaries had crossed the Atlantic to come face to face with a land that would change them completely. Arriving in Casablanca, Dorothy and I were overwhelmed, as my two parents must have been a half century earlier, by the sounds and smells of Morocco.

And the people of Morocco.

Not the wealthy, not the moneyed expatriates shopping in the chic stores of Casablanca, but the poor of Morocco.

From Casablanca, we took the train to Tangier.

There, thanks to an old missionary, we found the hospital in which a French nurse had once turned to my father and said, "Vous avez un fils!"

On the train back to Casablanca, the coast hugging our one side and the Great Atlantic holding the other flank, I slept the whole way, just as I had as a newborn in my mother's arms fifty years before, not crying once, to my mother's surprise.

We stepped off the train and walked around Casablanca.

Dorothy and I decided while in Casablanca to hunt down the old Rue Bugeaud, now named Zenqa Al Banafsaj, the street where Mom and Dad had studied Arabic and French, and where they had made their first attempts to convert Muslim Moroccans to Christianity. The address of the old building was fourteen Rue Bugeaud. Just off of the Boulevard Mohammad Zerktouni in Casablanca's town center. Fourteen Rue Bugeaud.

As we stood wondering how to get there, a voice cried out.

"Taxi, taxi!" We walked away, but the young taxi driver kept following us.

"Taxi, taxi," he kept saying. Finally, we agreed to hop in.

"La Rue Al Banafsaj, monsieur?" I asked. "Near the Boulevard Mohammad Zerktouni."

"Bien sûr, monsieur," he answered confidently, "Of course!"

Up and down we went, crisscrossing the Boulevard Mohammad Zerktouni. Nothing. The Rue Al Banafsaj had apparently disappeared.

"If you can't find it," I finally with exasperation, "then take us back to the hotel."

"Je vais le trouver, monsieur, je vais le trouver," he kept saying. "I will find it!"

He did find it. He kept driving around and asking people and eventually this taxi driver found the Rue Al Banafsaj, the old Rue Bugeaud. We then needed to find the number fourteen. Fourteen Rue Bugeaud.

Getting out of the taxi, I looked at the house numbers and suddenly, there it was, the number fourteen, and just above it, on this one building, the only building on the entire Rue Al Banafsaj, on this building where fifty years before my parents had started their  Moroccan journey, yes, there it was, the old street name sprawled out in large letters, as if waiting for me to find it. Fourteen, Rue Bugeaud.

From Casablanca we went to Rabat, and there saw the Quartier des Orangers where the Good News Bookstore, the "Maktaba al-bishara," had once peddled its evangelical wares in broad daylight.

Later that same day, we stood at the edge of the Bou Reg Reg River and stared across to the city of Salé where I had spent my last year in Morocco.

At one point during that week and a half in Morocco, we found ourselves in a small Berber village at the foot of the Middle Atlas Mountains. It was early in the afternoon on a cloudless day, the kind of day that occurs often in the Moroccan spring, when the heat is inescapable but the air is fresh and cool.

We walked the streets of the Berber village. We took in its houses with windows that stared out like sockets.

Everywhere we walked, children accompanied us, running in and out of street corners, offering us little things and asking for even littler things in return. I kept walking away.

"La, la, shoukran," was all I could say – "No, no, thank you." One boy started calling me "Monsieur La La Shoukran."

Dorothy, rather than resisting, let the children come close. She took it all in. She paused for two girls who handed her brightly colored tassels. The girls weren't looking for money. All they wanted in return was for us to stop and look at them.

Touched, Dorothy took the tassels and thanked them profusely.

Finally, I turned around and stopped to look at the tassels and the two girls who had given them.

And there, staring at their faces with smiles as free of clouds as the sky above me, I looked into their eyes and felt the love of God.

I did not know it then, but I had come home.

CPSIA information can be obtained
at www.ICGtesting.com
Printed in the USA
LVOW05s2256220118
563546LV00026B/563/P